# GARDEN RO

## FROM STILL BAY TO STORM

6 DISCOVER THE M

RESEARCHED, DEVELOPED
AND CREATED BY JACANA

 *Jacana*

# MESSAGES FROM CONSERVATION AND FORESTRY ORGANISATIONS

*Doringrivier Wilderness Area, Outeniqua Nature Reserve*

**DEPARTMENT OF WATER AFFAIRS AND FORESTRY**

## DEPARTMENT OF WATER AFFAIRS AND FORESTRY

The Forestry Chief Directorate of the Department of Water Affairs and Forestry manages 39 400 hectares of the approximately 60 500 hectares of indigenous forest in the southern Cap The approved policy for the indigenous forests is to manage these according to scientific principles and multiple-use considerations. The principle objectives are the maintenance of natural diversity and the sustainable use of forests for the benefit of all. This has a specific focus on the sustainable flow of benefits to communities, previously disadvantages by unfair discrimination, through their participation in sustainable forest management.

Timber harvesting is only carried out in 26% of the forest area. The remainder of the area either does not have sufficien marketable timber, or is too sensitive. The actual harvesting process is carried out in such a way as to minimise impact the environment and the harvesting system itself mimics the natural mortality rates and patterns of the forest thereby ensuring sustainability. Various types of recreational facilities are provided in the indigenous forest. Facilities include picninc sites, scenic drives, viewpoints, forest walks, hiking trails, mountain bike trails and horse trails. Other activities include ecological research, flora and fauna monitoring, weed control and law enforcement.

**SAFCOL**

## SOUTH AFRICAN FORESTRY COMPANY

This company is charged with the management and development of the State's investment in forestry and is dedicated to growing its business in the forestry and forestry products industr through technical, business and environmental excellence. SAFCOL strives to continually improve its environmental performance, and to this end is currently implementing ISO 1400 an environmental management system. SAFCOL was the first forestry company in the countr to be awarded the Forest Stewardship Council Certification, an international eco-labelling certificate aimed at linking informed customers with products manufactured in an environmentally sound fashion. SAFCOL takes a proactive approach to environmental impac

It strives to develop and promote a land stewardship ethic that integrates commercial forestry and other land-uses wi the conservation of renewable resources and the optimal use of non-renewable natural resources. In SAFCOL's continuing quest to lead the industry by example, the company strives to ensure that its activities are compatible wit the protection of the environment, hence promoting a green heritage for South Africa.

**South African NATIONAL PARKS**

## SOUTH AFRICAN NATIONAL PARKS

The Mission of the South African National Parks is to acquire and manage a system of National Parks that represents the indigenous wildlife, landscapes and significant cultural assets of South Africa for the pride and benefit of the nation. The South African National Par cannot fulfil this mission in an information vacuum. It is essential that the public supports th process, therefore they must be knowledgeable about the National Parks of South Africa, conservation objectives, and the need for specific actions or programmes.

**WESTERN CAPE NATURE CONSERVATION BOARD**

## WESTERN CAPE NATURE CONSERVATION BOARD

Western Cape Nature Conservation Board strives to conserve the biodiversity of the Western Cape by maintaining the natural resources of this beautiful province, and ensuring the sustainable utilisation of species and ecosystems. Western Cape Nature Conservation Board n only manages approximately 1 500 000 ha of land, but is actively involved with communities make these conservation areas more accessible to the public. The Board performs numerous functions, including the establishment and management of reserves and conservancies, communication with, and education of the public, and the enforcement of legislation for the protection and wise use of our natural resources.

# CONTENTS

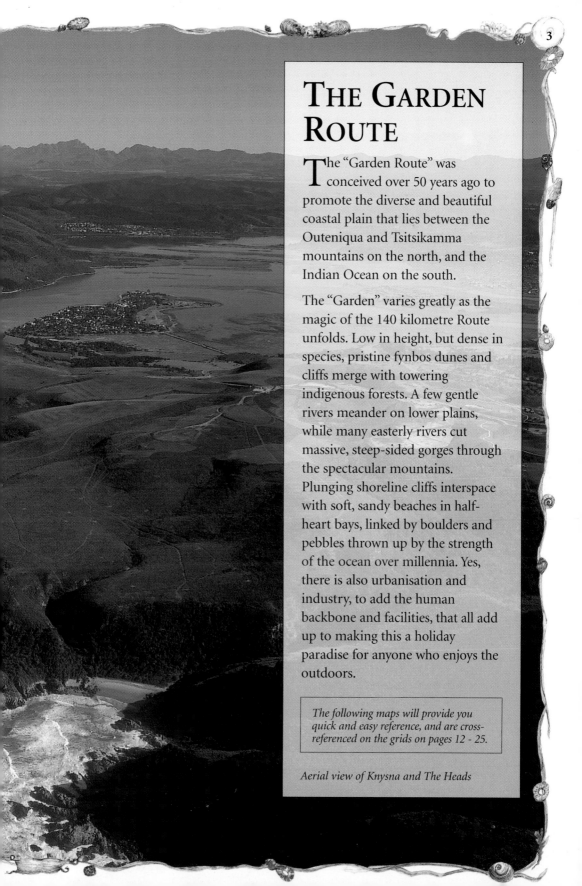

# THE GARDEN ROUTE

The "Garden Route" was conceived over 50 years ago to promote the diverse and beautiful coastal plain that lies between the Outeniqua and Tsitsikamma mountains on the north, and the Indian Ocean on the south.

The "Garden" varies greatly as the magic of the 140 kilometre Route unfolds. Low in height, but dense in species, pristine fynbos dunes and cliffs merge with towering indigenous forests. A few gentle rivers meander on lower plains, while many easterly rivers cut massive, steep-sided gorges through the spectacular mountains. Plunging shoreline cliffs interspace with soft, sandy beaches in half-heart bays, linked by boulders and pebbles thrown up by the strength of the ocean over millennia. Yes, there is also urbanisation and industry, to add the human backbone and facilities, that all add up to making this a holiday paradise for anyone who enjoys the outdoors.

*The following maps will provide you quick and easy reference, and are cross-referenced on the grids on pages 12 - 25.*

*Aerial view of Knysna and The Heads*

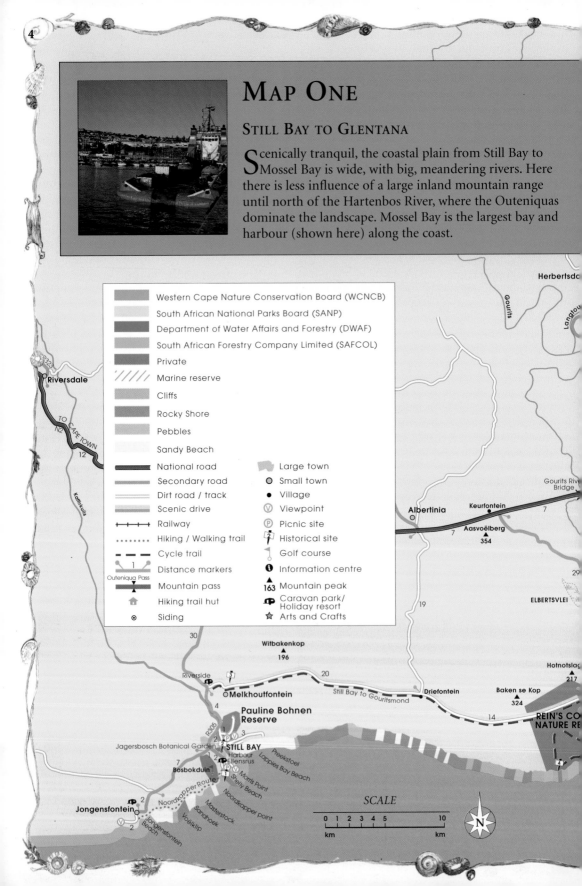

# MAP ONE

## STILL BAY TO GLENTANA

Scenically tranquil, the coastal plain from Still Bay to Mossel Bay is wide, with big, meandering rivers. Here there is less influence of a large inland mountain range until north of the Hartenbos River, where the Outeniquas dominate the landscape. Mossel Bay is the largest bay and harbour (shown here) along the coast.

**Legend:**

- Western Cape Nature Conservation Board (WCNCB)
- South African National Parks Board (SANP)
- Department of Water Affairs and Forestry (DWAF)
- South African Forestry Company Limited (SAFCOL)
- Private
- Marine reserve
- Cliffs
- Rocky Shore
- Pebbles
- Sandy Beach
- National road
- Secondary road
- Dirt road / track
- Scenic drive
- Railway
- Hiking / Walking trail
- Cycle trail
- Distance markers
- Mountain pass
- Hiking trail hut
- Siding
- Large town
- Small town
- Village
- Viewpoint
- Picnic site
- Historical site
- Golf course
- Information centre
- Mountain peak
- 163 Mountain peak
- Caravan park/ Holiday resort
- Arts and Crafts

Herbertsdc

Gourits

Langlou

Riversdale

TO CAPE TOWN
N2

12

Kaffirkuils

Gourits Rive Bridge

Albertinia

Keurfontein

Aasvoëlberg
354

7

7

29

ELBERTSVLEI

19

30

Witbakenkop
▲ 196

Riverside

Melkhoutfontein

20

Still Bay to Gouritsmond

Driefontein

Baken se Kop
▲ 324

14

Hotnotslac
▲ 217

REIN'S CO
NATURE RE

Pauline Bohnen Reserve

4

Jagersbosch Botanical Garden

STILL BAY

R305

3

2

Harbour
Ellensrus

Preekstoel

Lappies Bay Beach

7

Bosbokduin

Morris Point

Shelly Beach

Noordkapper Route

Noordkapper point

Masterstock

Sandhoek

Jongensfontein

2

Voëlklip

Jongensfontein Beach

2

SCALE

0 1 2 3 4 5      10

km      km

N

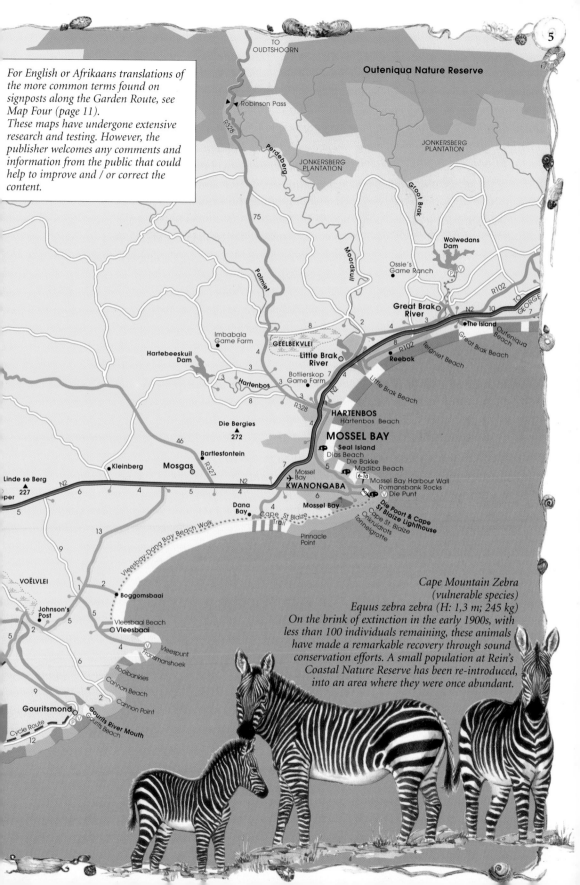

TO
OUDTSHOORN

Outeniqua Nature Reserve

For English or Afrikaans translations of
the more common terms found on
signposts along the Garden Route, see
Map Four (page 11).
These maps have undergone extensive
research and testing. However, the
publisher welcomes any comments and
information from the public that could
help to improve and / or correct the
content.

Robinson Pass

R328

Perdeberg

JONKERSBERG
PLANTATION

JONKERSBERG
PLANTATION

Groot Brak

Moordkuil

Wolwedans
Dam

75

Palmiet

Ossie's
Game Ranch

R102

TO
GEORGE

Great Brak
River

N2

10

7

Imbabala
Game Farm

GEELBEKVLEI

8

2

4

3

The Island

Outeniqua
Beach

Great Brak Beach

Hartebeeskuil
Dam

Little Brak
River

Botlierskop
Game Farm

7

Reebok

R102

Tergniet Beach

Little Brak Beach

3

3

Hartenbos

4

8

R328

4

HARTENBOS

Hartenbos Beach

Die Bergies
▲
272

46

Bartlesfontein

4

MOSSEL BAY

Seal Island

Dias Beach
Die Bakke
Madiba Beach

Kleinberg

Mosgas

R327

7

Mossel
Bay

5

6-10

Mossel Bay Harbour Wall
Romansbank Rocks

Linde se Berg
▲
227

N2

N2

KWANONQABA

6

Die Punt

per

6

4

Mossel Bay

Die Poort & Cape
St Blaize Lighthouse

5

Dana
Bay

4

Cape St Blaize

Onkruidrots

Tonnelgrotte

13

Cape
Trail

St Blaize

Pinnacle
Point

9

Vleesbaai-Dana Bay Beach Walk

VOËLVLEI

1

2

Boggomsbaai

*Cape Mountain Zebra*
*(vulnerable species)*
*Equus zebra zebra (H: 1,3 m; 245 kg)*
*On the brink of extinction in the early 1900s, with*
*less than 100 individuals remaining, these animals*
*have made a remarkable recovery through sound*
*conservation efforts. A small population at Rein's*
*Coastal Nature Reserve has been re-introduced,*
*into an area where they were once abundant.*

Johnson's
Post

5

5

2

Vleesbaai Beach

O Vleesbaai

5

2

4

Vleespunt

Transmanshoek

6

Rodibankies

9

Cannon Beach

2

Cannon Point

Gouritsmond

Gourits River Mouth

Cycle Route

Gourits Beach

12

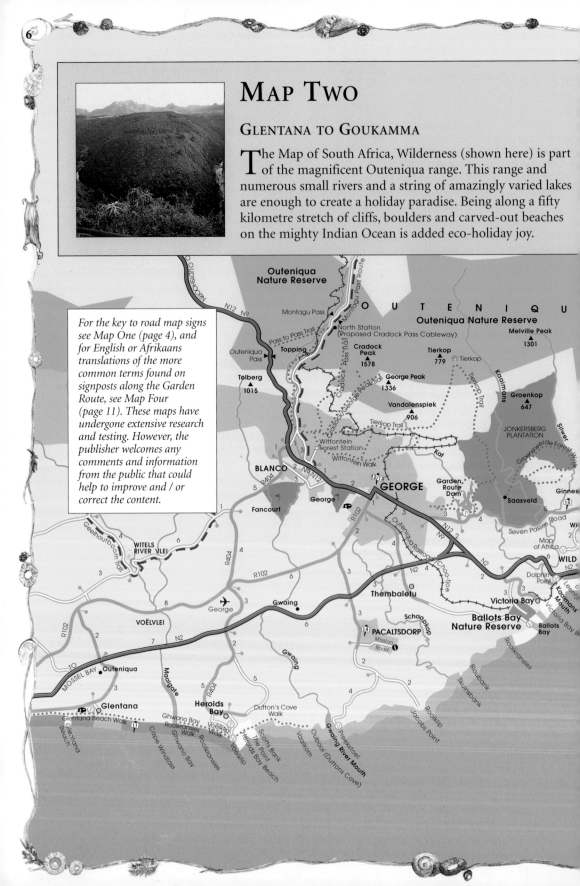

# MAP TWO

## GLENTANA TO GOUKAMMA

The Map of South Africa, Wilderness (shown here) is part of the magnificent Outeniqua range. This range and numerous small rivers and a string of amazingly varied lakes are enough to create a holiday paradise. Being along a fifty kilometre stretch of cliffs, boulders and carved-out beaches on the mighty Indian Ocean is added eco-holiday joy.

*For the key to road map signs see Map One (page 4), and for English or Afrikaans translations of the more common terms found on signposts along the Garden Route, see Map Four (page 11). These maps have undergone extensive research and testing. However, the publisher welcomes any comments and information from the public that could help to improve and / or correct the content.*

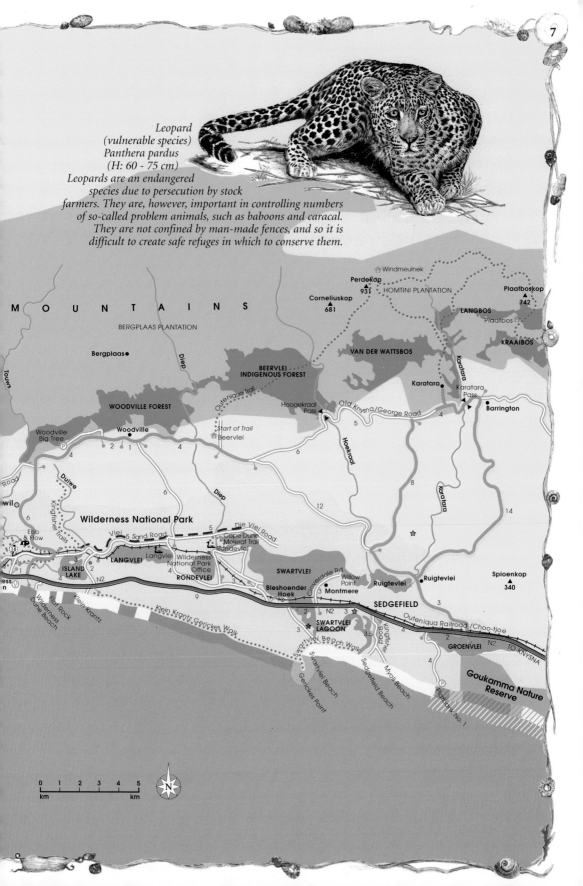

Leopard
(vulnerable species)
*Panthera pardus*
(H: 60 - 75 cm)
Leopards are an endangered
species due to persecution by stock
farmers. They are, however, important in controlling numbers
of so-called problem animals, such as baboons and caracal.
They are not confined by man-made fences, and so it is
difficult to create safe refuges in which to conserve them.

M O U N T A I N S

BERGPLAAS PLANTATION

Bergplaas●

Windmeulnek

Perdekop
931

HOMTINI PLANTATION

Plaatboskop
742

Corneliuskop
681

LANGBOS

Plaatbos

BEERVLEI
INDIGENOUS FOREST

VAN DER WATTSBOS

KRAAIBOS

WOODVILLE FOREST

Diep

Outeniqua Trail

Hoogekraal
Pass

Old Knysna/George Road

Karatara

Karatara●

Karatara
Pass

Barrington

Woodville
Big Tree

Woodville

Start of Trail
Beervlei

4

Touws

Road

Duiwe

2    1

4

6

5

Hoekraal

6

8

wil○

Kingfisher Trails

Diep

12

Karatara

14

Wilderness National Park

Die Vlei Road

Vlei   5  Sand Road        5

Cape Dune
Molerat Trail
Rondevlei

☆

Ebb
& Flow

16

LANGVLEI

Langvlei

Wilderness
National Park
Office

SWARTVLEI

Willow
Point

Ruigtevlei

Ruigtevlei

Spioenkop
340

ISLAND
LAKE

2

RONDEVLEI

N2

3

Bleshoender
Hoek

Cloveraale Rd

3  Montmere

SEDGEFIELD

3

ess

Flat Rock

Klein Krantz

Wilderness
Dune Beach

Klein Krantz Gerickes Walk

9

2

N2   3  ☆

SWARTVLEI
LAGOON

Swartvlei Beach Walk

3.5

Kingfisher
Road

Outeniqua Railroad /Choo-tjoe

GROENVLEI

2

N2

TO KNYSNA

Swartvlei Beach

Gerickes Point

Sedgefield Beach

Myoli Beach

4

P

Platform No. 1

Goukamma Nature
Reserve

0   1   2   3   4   5
km                   km

N

# MAP THREE

## GOUKAMMA TO PLETTENBERG BAY

Renowned for its nearby mountains, forests, human history and lagoon, the Knysna area has been a lifestyle and tourist destination for over a century. Holiday-makers return to the same spots decade after decade, especially to the Knysna Heads (western head shown here).

*For the key to road map signs see Map One (page 4), and for English or Afrikaans translations of the more common terms found on signposts along the Garden Route, see Map Four (page 11).*

(M)

(M)

Under-side

The Brenton Copper
butterflies are extremely rare
and endangered, and are
only found at Brenton-on-Sea.
They have a close relationship with
the Cock-tail Ant. The ant feeds on
secretions from the honey gland, and
in return the ants protect the larvae.
The Brenton Blue butterflies only
occur at Brenton-on-Sea Reserve.

Brenton
Copper
(threatened species
and endemic)
*Chrysoritis mithras*
(24 - 28 mm)

renton Blue
hreatened species
~ endemic)
Drachrysops niobe
9 - 32 mm)

SOETKRAAL
WILDERNESS AREA

R339
TO PRINCE ALFREDS PASS

Kruisvallei

R339

Keurbooms

R340

9

Buffelsnek
Forest Station

Ysternek
Nature
Reserve

BUFFELSNEK
PLANTATION

Kransbos
Forest
Station

The Elephant
Trails

Diepwalle
Forest Station

Perdekop
▲
729

Tarkaberg
▲
579

JAKKALSKRAAL MOUNTAINS

WYNANDSKRAAL MOUNTAINS

Keurbooms

Malvarug
▲
511

Palmiet

Spitskop
▲
627

KEURBOOMSRIVER
PLANTATION

14

Keurbooms

Whiskey Creek
Nature Reserve

Keurbooms

Keurbooms River
Nature
Reserve

Hartbees

TO STORMS RIVER

Ouengtqa Trail

Petrus se Brand Trail

DIEPWALLE INDIGENOUS FOREST

Fisantehoek

Stinkhout Draai

HESENS
NOUS FOREST
LANTATION

Witels

Garden
of Eden

6

Harkerville Routes

HARKERVILLE
Harkerville
Forest Station

Kranshoek

cken Hill
ls

Sinclair
Nature
Reserve

HARKERVILLE
FOREST

Sinclair

Harkerville Trail

Grootkop

Mouth

Stevens Bank

Romansgat

Walk

Kranshoek

Kranshoek

3

8

2

Plettenberg
Bay

Kranshoek

Roojkrans

Ghwanqpad

Stilbaai

N2

Knysna
Elephant Park

Bitou

Wittedrift

R340

5

Bitou

Wittedrift
Trails

8

New
Horizons

Kwanakhatula

Piesang

2

Weldon
House

N2

2

2

Goose
Valley

Stanley's
Island

KEURBOOMS
LAGOON

Breeding
Colony

Keurbooms Beach

4

N2

2

Piesang
Valley

32-38

Lookout Beach
Lookout Rocks
The Wedge
Hoble Beach
Central Beach
Beacon Island Rocks
Robberg Beacon Island Beach

28

Plettenberg
Bay

PLETTENBERG BAY
Robberg 5

Robberg
Corner

Meirle Bank
The Gap
Kamonakoei Gat

30

Robberg
Nature Reserve

Robberg
trails

The
Island

The
Ledge

Whale Rock

The
Point

Nelson Bay

Plaatbank No. 2

Robberg
P. trails

Robberg Beach

27

0  1  2  3  4  5
km                    km

N

# Map Four

## Plettenberg Bay to Storms River

Arguably the most beautiful part of the Garden Route, the world famous Plettenberg Bay and Keurbooms Lagoon make this coastal stretch South Africa's premier holiday resort with all the facilities that this entails. Despite this, the true outdoor-lover has literally thousands of venues to explore far from the human noise and bustle, like the De Vasselot Nature Reserve (shown here).

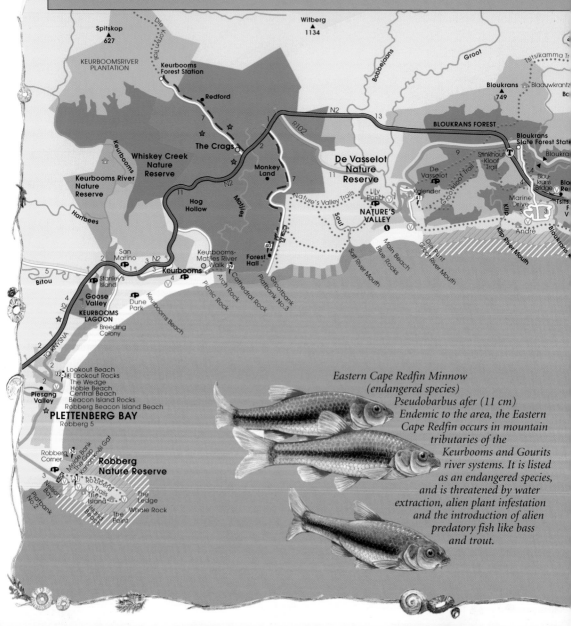

*Eastern Cape Redfin Minnow
(endangered species)
Pseudobarbus afer (11 cm)
Endemic to the area, the Eastern
Cape Redfin occurs in mountain
tributaries of the
Keurbooms and Gourits
river systems. It is listed
as an endangered species,
and is threatened by water
extraction, alien plant infestation
and the introduction of alien
predatory fish like bass
and trout.*

For the key to road map signs see Map One (page 4). These maps have undergone extensive research and testing. However, the publisher welcomes any comments and information from the public that could help to improve and / or correct the content.

The following terms are common on signposts along the Garden Route:

| Afrikaans | English |
|---|---|
| Berg | Mountain |
| Rivier | River |
| Baai | Bay |
| Mond | Mouth |
| Strand | Beach |
| Groot | Great, Large |
| Klein | Little, Small |
| Woud | Forest |
| Punt | Point |
| Boom | Tree |
| Brug | Bridge |
| Tuin | Garden |
| Wildtuin | Game Reserve/ National Park |

# THINGS TO DO, PLACES TO VISIT

The grids on these pages have been designed in conjunction with the maps on pages 4 - 11. Each grid is coded with different bands of colour relating respectively to Maps 1 - 4. The entries on the grids appear in order of their geographical position on the map, reading from left to right. Whatever magic you are hoping to discover along the Garden Route, these grids will help you to access the best that the area has to offer.

## KEY TO MAP COLOURS

**Map 1**
(pages 4 - 5)

**Map 2**
(pages 6 - 7)

**Map 3**
(pages 8 - 9)

**Map 4**
(pages 10 - 11)

## CONTENTS

## KEY TO AUTHORITIES

ABM – Albertinia Municipality
DWAF – Dept. of Water Affairs and Forestry
GBM – Great Brak Municipality
GM – George Municipality
KM – Knysna Municipality
MBM – Mossel Bay Municipality
MBP – Mossel Bay Port
NV – Nature's Valley
P – Private
PBM – Plettenberg Bay Municipality
SAF – SAFCOL
SANP – South African National Parks
SBM – Still Bay Municipality
SM – Sedgefield Municipality
WCNCB – Western Cape Nature Conservation Board
WM – Wilderness Municipality
WT – Wilderness Tourism

*Please note that telephone numbers do change. For further information or clarification, consult the local telephone directories or contact 1023 for directory assistance. The publishers welcome feedback from users of these pages.*

## INFORMATION CENTRES

| LOCATION | TEL. NO. |
|---|---|
| Western Cape Tourism Board | 021 – 426 5639 |
| South African National Parks | 021 – 422 2810/6 |
| Still Bay | 028 – 754 2602 |
| Mossel Bay | 044 – 691 2202 |
| Great Brak | 044 – 620 2100 |
| George | 044 – 801 9295 |
| Wilderness | 044 – 877 0045 |
| Sedgefield | 044 – 343 2658 |
| Knysna | 044 – 382 5510 |
| Plettenberg Bay | 044 – 533 4065 |
|  | 044 – 533 3732 |
| Bloukrans Bridge | 042 – 281 1458 |
| Storms River | 042 – 750 3563 |

## AIRLINES SERVICING THE GARDEN ROUTE

| LOCATION | TEL.NO. |
|---|---|
| Sabena-Nationwide: | |
| George | 044 – 801 8412 |
| SA Airlink: | |
| George | 044 – 801 8410 |
| Plettenberg Bay | 044 – 533 9041 |
| SAA: | |
| George | 044 – 801 8448 |

## CAR RENTALS

| LOCATION | | TEL. NO. |
|---|---|---|
| Budget: | | |
| George | town | 044 – 873 6259 |
|  | airport | 044 – 876 9204 |
|  |  | 044 – 876 9216 |
| Plettenberg Bay | | 044 – 533 2197 |
| Avis: | | |
| George | airport | 044 – 876 9314 |
| Plettenberg Bay | | 044 – 533 1315 |
| Imperial: | | |
| George | | 044 – 876 9017 |
| Plettenberg Bay | | 044 – 533 3176 |
|  |  | 083 244 4321 |

*Erica versicolor (page 90) is one of the special fynbos plants.*

## DISTANCE GRID

This table summarises the distances and travelling times between major centres, driving along tar roads only. Travelling times are estimated at an average of 100 km/hr.

| TOWNS | DISTANCE | TIME |
|---|---|---|
| Still Bay to Gouritsmond | 109 km | 1 hour 10 min |
| Still Bay to Mossel Bay | 113 km | 1 hour 25 min |
| Gouritsmond to Mossel Bay | 80 km | 1 hour |
| Mossel Bay to George | 45 km | 30 minutes |
| Mossel Bay to Wilderness | 54 km | 40 minutes |
| George to Wilderness | 16 km | 15 minutes |
| Wilderness to Sedgefield | 22 km | 15 minutes |
| Sedgefield to Knysna | 36 km | 25 minutes |
| Knysna to Plettenberg Bay | 32 km | 25 minutes |
| Plettenberg Bay to Natures Valley | 37 km | 30 minutes |
| Plettenberg Bay to Storms River | 74 km | 45 minutes |
| Nature's Valley to Storms River | 45 km | 30 minutes |

*The Cape Sugarbird (page 122) is an endemic bird to fynbos and the area.*

*Fynbos in full colour*

14

# CARAVAN SITES

*Indicates Restaurant/Kiosk only open
in December.

| LOCATION | TEL. NO. | Restaurant/Kiosk | Swimming Pool | AUTH |
|---|---|---|---|---|
| Jongersfontein | 028 – 754 8015 | | | SBM |
| Riverside | 028 – 754 1608 | • | | P |
| Ellensrus | 028 – 754 1034 | | | SBM |
| Dias Beach | 044 – 692 0020 | | | MBM |
| De Bakke/Santos Caravan Park | 044 – 691 2915 | | | MBM |
| Die Punt Caravan Park | 044 – 690 3501 | | | MBM |
| Glentana | 044 – 879 1536 | | | P |
| George Tourist Resort | 044 – 874 5205 | • | • | P |
| Ebb and Flow (Wilderness) | 044 – 877 1197 | • | | WM |
| Woodbourne (Knysna) | 044 – 384 0316 | | | P |
| Monks (Knysna) | 044 – 382 2609 | | • | P |
| Lake Brenton (Knysna) | 044 – 381 0060 | | • | P |
| Keurbooms Lagoon (Plett) | 044 – 533 2567 | | | P |
| San Marino Holiday Resort | 044 – 535 9700 | | | P |
| Aventura Eco Plettenberg | 044 – 535 9309 | | • | P |
| Dune Park Holiday Resorts | 044 – 535 9606 | • | • | P |
| Arch Rock | 044 – 535 9409 | | | P |
| Robberg Caravan Park | 044 – 533 2571 | | | P |
| Lily Pond (The Crags) | 044 – 534 8767 | • | | NV |
| De Vasselot Holiday Resort | 044 – 531 6700 | | | SANP |
| Storms River Mouth | 042 – 541 1607 | | | SANP |

*A forested drive between Knysna and George*

# SCENIC ROUTES AND DRIVES

The entire Garden Route is scenic, however we have listed
below the most spectacular short or day trips. Refer to the
maps (pages 4 - 11) for distances. * Indicates picnic spots.

| NAME/ROUTE | COMMENTS |
|---|---|
| The Outeniqua Choo-tjoe, George to Knysna | Relaxing coastal route by steam train Tel.no. 044-801-8288 |
| Still Bay to Gourits River Mouth | Unusual coastline, exquisite fynbos, old architecture |
| *The Outeniqua Pass, Oudtshoorn to George | Spectacular mountain views, built 1943-1951 |
| *The Montagu Pass, Oudtshoorn to George | Original ox-wagon pass, built 1844-1848 |
| *The Seven Passes, George to Knysna | Mountain, country and indigenous forests |
| *The Old Cape Road to Kom se Pad, Knysna | Mountain and indigenous forests |
| *R339: Prince Alfred's Pass, Knysna to Diepwalle | Indigenous forests, good view spot at Spitskop, 933 m high |
| Stinkhout Draai, 2 km east of Garden of Eden | Indigenous forest drive |
| *Harkerville to Kranshoek, Plettenberg Bay | Indigenous forests, coastal view spot |
| *R340: Plettenberg Bay to Kruisvallei | Excellent vantage point to view the Tsitsikamma and Wynandskraal Mnts. |
| *R102: Grootrivier Pass, Nature's Valley | Indigenous forests, valleys and sightings of ancient yellowwood trees. |
| *Marine Drive, Turn off R102 at Bloukrans Forestry Station | Circular drive, panoramic views of Storms River to Plettenberg Bay and Formosa Peak |
| *R102: Bloukrans Pass | Indigenous forests and valleys |

*Vervet Monkeys (page
102) are occasionally
spotted along the
roadside and at caravan
parks, in forested areas.
Please do not feed these
or any other wild
animals.*

*Most places along the Garden Route can be easily accessed by car. Don't forget your sunglasses!*

*The entries on the grids appear in order of their geographical position on the map, reading from left to right.*

## EASY-TO-ACCESS INDIGENOUS VEGETATION

These places can be visited either by car, or by a short, easy walk. A beautiful gum-tree plantation and information display at Bracken Hill Falls is worth visiting.

## ECO-ADVENTURE TOURS

| LAUNCH SITES | TEL. NO. | AUTH. |
|---|---|---|
| Eco Bound | 044 – 871 4455 | P |
| Outeniqua Adventure Tours | 044 – 871 1470 | P |
| Eden Adventures | 044 – 877 0179 | P |
| Eco-Afrika Tours | 082 925 0716 | P |
| Knysna Elephant Park | 044 – 532 7732 | P |
| Monkeyland | 044 – 534 8906 | P |

| LOCATION | Dune Vegetation | Estuary | Forest | Fynbos |
|---|---|---|---|---|
| Geelkrans Nature Reserve | | | | • |
| Rein's Coastal Nature Reserve | | | | • |
| Ballots Bay | | | | • |
| Seven Passes | | | • | • |
| Pledge Nature Reserve | | | | • |
| R339 to Knoetze | | | • | • |
| Kranshoek | | | • | • |
| Robberg Gate Car Park | | | | • |
| R340 (Wittedrift - Kruisvalley) | | | | • |
| Heidehof (The Crags) | | | | • |
| R102 (Off N2 Natures Valley - Road to Platbank No 3) | • | | | • |
| Nature's Valley Town | | | | • |
| Tsitsikamma Lodge | | | • | • |
| N2 Tollgate (Stormsriver) | | | • | |
| Garden of Eden | | | • | |
| Aventura Eco Plettenberg Holiday Resort | | | • | |
| Forest Hall | | | | • |
| Goosemarsh | | • | | |

## PARKS, RESERVES AND GAME FARMS

There are a number of conserved areas along the Garden Route. See pages 102 - 105 for more information on land mammals.

*Indicates the presence of the larger mammals.

| LOCATION | TEL. NO. | AUTH. |
|---|---|---|
| Pauline Bohnen Reserve | 028 – 754 2602 | SBM |
| *Rein's Coastal Nature Reserve | 028 – 735 3322 | P |
| Imbabala Game Farm | 044 – 695 2767 | P |
| Zingela Indlela Game Tracks | 044 – 694 0011 | P |
| Botlierskop Game Farm | 044 – 696 6055 | P |
| Ossie's Game Ranch | 044 – 620 2275 | P |
| Outeniqua Nature Reserve | 044 – 870 8323 | WCNCB |
| Ballots Bay Nature Reserve | 044 – 880 1153 | P |
| Goukamma Nature Reserve | 044 – 383 0042 | WCNCB |
| *Featherbed Nature Reserve | 044 – 382 1693 | P |
| Ysterhout Rug | 044 – 382 5466 | DWAF |
| Robberg Nature Reserve | 044 – 533 2125 | WCNCB |
| Keurbooms Nature Reserve | 044 – 533 2125 | WCNCB |
| Hog Hollow | 044 – 534 8769 | P |
| Lily Pond | 044 – 534 8767 | P |
| De Vasselot Nature Reserve | 042 – 531 6700 | NPB |
| Tsitsikamma National Park | 042 – 541 1607 | SANP |
| Plaatbos Nature Reserve | 042 – 541 1557 | DWAF |

*Rein's Coastal Nature Reserve*

*Bontebok (page 103)*

# BIRDING

The Garden Route is famous for its birds. The listed places tend to be most rewarding, and are easily accessible. See pages 118 - 129 for more information.

*Binoculars and field note book are handy for recording observations.*

| LOCATION | Coastal | Forest | Fynbos | Estuary/Inland Water | Mountain | River | AUTH |
|---|---|---|---|---|---|---|---|
| Pauline Bohnen Nature Reserve | • | • | | | | | P |
| Geelkrans Walk | • | • | | | | | WCNCB |
| Rein's Coastal Nature Reserve | • | • | | | | | P |
| Elbertsvlei | | | | • | | | P |
| Voëlvlei | | | | • | | | P |
| Gourits Mouth | • | | | • | | • | M |
| Seal Island | • | | | | | | PT |
| Haartebeeskuil Dam | | | | • | | | MBP |
| Geelbekvlei | | | | • | | | MBP |
| Little Brak Estuary | • | | | • | | | MBP |
| Garden Route Dam | | • | | | • | • | GM |
| Ballots Bay | • | • | • | | | • | P |
| Groeneweide Forest Walk | | • | | | • | • | DWAF |
| Outeniqua Hiking trail | | • | • | | • | • | DWAF |
| Kingfisher Trails | • | • | • | • | | • | SANP |
| Cape Dune Molerat | | • | | | | • | SANP |
| Langvlei Hide | • | | | | | • | SANP |
| Rondevlei Hide | • | | | | | • | SANP |
| Willow Point | • | | | | | • | SANP |
| Groenvlei | | | • | • | | | WCNCB |
| Goukamma Nature Reserve | • | | • | • | | • | WCNCB |
| Buffalo Valley Game Farm | • | | | | | | P |
| Belvidere Manor | • | • | • | • | | | P |
| Jubillee Creek Walk | | • | | | • | • | DWAF |
| Lielievlei Nature Reserve | | • | • | | | • | DWAF |
| Pledge Nature Reserve | | | • | | | | KM |
| Featherbed Nature Reserve | • | • | | • | | | P |
| Leisure Island | • | | | | | | P |
| Woodbourne Pan | • | | | • | | • | P |
| Knoetzie | • | | | • | • | • | DWAF |
| The Elephant Trails | | • | | | • | • | DWAF |
| Garden of Eden | | • | | | | | DWAF |
| Harkerville | • | • | • | | • | • | DWAF |
| Wittedrift Nature Trails | • | • | • | • | • | • | PBM |
| Robberg Reserve | • | | • | • | | | WCNCB |
| Aventura Eco Plettenberg | | • | | • | | • | P |
| Piesang River | • | | | • | | • | PBM |
| Bitou River | • | | | • | | | PBM |
| Keurbooms River Breeding Colony | • | | | | | | WCNCB |
| Keurbooms Nature Reserve | • | • | • | | | • | WCNCB |
| De Vasselot Nature Reserve | • | • | • | • | • | • | SANP |
| Tsitsikamma National Park | • | • | • | • | • | • | SANP |
| Plaatbos Nature Reserve | | • | | | | • | DWAF |

## BIRD CLUBS

| LOCATION | TEL. NO. |
|---|---|
| The Lakes Bird Club (Still Bay, Mossel Bay, George, Wilderness, Sedgefield, Knysna) | 044 – 871 2677 |
| Plettenberg Bay | 044 – 533 0099 |

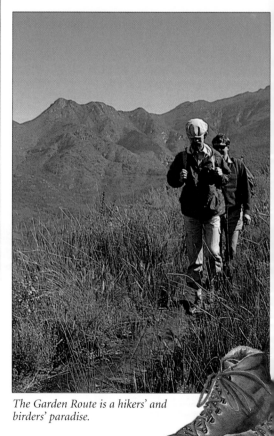

*The Whimbrel (page 119) is one of many special water birds that can be viewed along the Garden Route.*

*The Garden Route is a hikers' and birders' paradise.*

# Hiking and Walking

The entire region is a paradise for hiking. The trails listed are the most accessible, well-marked and maintained. Please refer to the authority indicated for permits and information. SI = Self issued
* Indicates permits needed in school holidays only.

*Key-hole limpets (page 79)*

| LOCATION | TEL. NO. | DISTANCE | GRADING | PERMIT | Coastal | Forest | Fynbos | Estuary | River | Mountain | AUTH |
|---|---|---|---|---|:-:|:-:|:-:|:-:|:-:|:-:|---|
| Sleeping Beauty Trail | 028 – 713 2418 | 13 km | Difficult | Yes | • | • | • | | | • | P |
| Crystal Kloof | 028 –713 2418 | 21 km (2 days) | Easy | Yes | | • | • | | | | RM |
| Noordkapper Route | 028 – 754 2602 | 11 km | Easy | No | • | | | | | | SBM |
| Pauline Bohnen | 028 – 754 2602 | Differs | Varies | No | | | • | | | | SBM |
| Strandloper Trail | 028 – 754 2602 | 9 km | Easy | No | | | • | | | | SBM |
| Wesoewer Trail | 028 – 754 2602 | 3 km | Easy | No | | | • | | | | SBM |
| Rein's Coastal Nature Reserve | 028 – 735 3322 | 6 km | Easy | No | • | | • | | | | P |
| Cape St Blaize Trail | 044 – 691 2202 | 15 km | Mod | No | • | | • | | | • | MBM |
| Eight Bell Mountain Inn | 044 – 631 0000 | 5 km | Varies | No | | • | • | • | | | P |
| Glentana Beach Walk | 044 – 873 6314 | 6 km | Easy | No | • | | | | | | GM |
| Ghwano Bay to Rooikransies | 044 – 873 6314 | 4 km | Easy | No | • | | | | | | GM |
| Voëlklip to Herolds Bay | 044 – 873 6314 | 4 km | Easy | No | • | | | | | | GM |
| Herolds Bay to Scotts Bank | 044 – 873 6314 | 4 km | Easy | No | • | | | | | | GM |
| Duttons Cove Walk | 044 – 873 6314 | 4km | Easy | No | • | | • | | | | GM |
| Cradock Pass Trail | 044 – 870 8323 | 12 km | Difficult | SI | | • | | | | • | WCNCB |
| Pass to Pass Trail | 044 – 870 8323 | 7 km | Varies | SI | | • | | | | • | WCNCB |
| Cradock/George Peak Trail | 044 – 870 8323 | 18 km | Difficult | SI | | | • | | | • | WCNCB |
| Tierkop Hiking Trail | 044 – 870 8323 | 14 km | Mod | Yes | | • | | | | • | WCNCB |
| Witfontein Forest Walks | 044 – 870 8323 | Varies | Easy | SI | | • | | | | | WCNCB |
| Groeneweide Forest Walks | 044 – 801 9295 | Varies | Varies | SI | | • | | | | | DWAF |
| Kingfisher Trails | 044 – 877 0784 | Varies | Varies | No | | • | | | • | • | SANP |
| Cape Dune Molerat Trail | 044 – 877 0784 | 8 km | Easy | No | | | • | | • | | SANP |
| Klein Krantz to Gerickes Point | 044 – 877 0784 | 14 km | Easy | No | • | | | | | | SANP |
| Swartvlei Beach Walk | 044 – 877 0784 | 5 km | Mod | No | • | | | | | | SANP |
| Outeniqua Trail | 044 – 382 5466 | 108 km | Mod/Diff | Yes | | • | • | | • | • | DWAF |
| Attaquas Trail | 044 – 382 8323 | Differs | Difficult | Yes | | | • | | | • | WCNCB |
| Goukamma Beach Walk | 044 – 343 2658 | 14 km | Easy | No | • | | | | | | SM |
| *Jubilee Creek Walk | 044 – 382 5466 | 4 km | Easy | No | | • | | | • | | DWAF |
| *Millwood Mine Walk | 044 – 382 5466 | 5.6 km | Mod | *No | | • | • | | | | DWAF |
| Buffalo to Brenton Beach Walk | 044 – 382 2095 | 7 km | Easy | No | • | | | | | | WCNCB |
| *Terblans Walk | 044 –382 5466 | 7 km | Easy | *No | | • | | | | | DWAF |
| *The Elephant Trails | 044 – 382 5466 | Differs | Varies | *No | | • | | | | | DWAF |
| *Garden of Eden | 044 – 382 5466 | 1 km | Easy | No | | • | | | | | DWAF |
| Harkerville Coastal Trail | 044 – 382 5466 | 26 km | Difficult | Yes | • | • | • | | • | | DWAF |
| Kranshoek Walk | 044 – 382 5466 | 9 km | Mod/Diff | No | • | • | • | | | | DWAF |
| Bracken Hill Waterfalls | 044 – 375 0243 | Differs | Varies | No | | • | | | • | | SAF |
| Wittedrift Nature Trails | 044 – 533 2125 | Differs | Easy/Diff | No | | • | • | | • | | WCNCB |
| Pristine Discoveries – Guided Walks | 044 – 533 5970 082 954 1314 | Differs | Varies | Yes | | | | | | | P |
| Robberg Guided Walks | 044 – 533 3732 | Differs | Varies | Yes | • | • | • | | | • | WCNCB |
| Robberg Natures Reserve | 044 – 533 2125 | Differs | Varies | Yes | • | • | • | | | • | WCNCB |
| Keurbooms – Matjies River Walk | 044 – 533 3732 | 3 km | Mod | No | • | | | | • | | P |
| Keurbooms Forestry Station | 044 – 534 8720 | Differs | Easy | Yes | | • | | | • | | SAF |
| Nature Valley Trails (Refer to De Vasselot Camp Site for permit and maps) | 044 – 531 6700 | Differs | Varies | Yes | • | • | • | • | • | | SANP |
| Tsitsikamma Hiking Trail | 042 – 391 0393 | 61 km | Mod | Yes | | • | • | | • | • | SANP |
| Stinkhoutkloof Trail | 042 – 541 1557 | 8.4 km | Difficult | SI | | • | | | • | | DWAF |
| Rugbos Trails | 042 – 541 1557 | Differs | Varies | SI | | • | • | | • | • | DWAF |
| Plaatbos Trails | 042 – 541 1557 | Differs | Mod | SI | | • | • | | • | | DWAF |
| Otter Trail | 012 – 343 1991 | 48 km | Difficult | Yes | • | • | • | | • | | SANP |
| Dolphin Trail | 042 – 750 3818 | 20 km | Easy/Mod | Yes | | | | | | | SANP |
| Storms River Mouth Trails (Refer to Storms River Mouth office for permits and maps) | 042 – 541 1607 | Differs | Varies | No | • | • | • | | • | | SANP |

*A good pair of hiking boots or walking shoes are advised.*

# HISTORICAL SITES

Read about the human history on pages 132 - 145. The numbers next to each location appear on the maps. The following themes are marked:

| EH | = | Early History, pages 128 - 131 |
|---|---|---|
| TES | = | Travellers & Early Settlers, pages 132 - 133 |
| NTC | = | Nineteenth & Twentieth Centuries, pages 134 - 137 |

| NO. ON MAP | LOCATION | HISTORY | THEME |
|---|---|---|---|
| 1 | Fish Traps | 59 | EH |
| 2 | Pallinggat Homestead | 62 | NTC |
| 3 | Melkhoutfontein | 60 | TES |
| 4 | Rein's Nature Reserve Gouriqua | 59 | EH |
| 5 | St Blaize Lighthouse | 60 | TES |
| 6 | Bats Cave | 59 | EH |
| 7 | Cape St Blaize Cave | 58 | EH |
| 8 | Bartolomeu Diaz Centre | 60 | TES |
| 9 | Post Office Tree | 61 | TES |
| 10 | Historical Walk | 62 | NTC |
| 11 | Floating Dock Wreck, 2 km east Glentana | 60 | TES |
| 12 | Walking Tour, George | 62 | NTC |
| 13 | Tree & Timber Museum | 60 | TES |
| 14 | Pacaltsdorp Stone Church Captain Dikkop's Grave 2 roomed cottage Patat Huisie | 60 | TES |
| 15 | Seven Passes Road | 60 | TES |
| 16 | Ebb and Flow Cave, near Wilderness | 58 | EH |
| 17 | Portland Manor Estate | 62 | NTC |
| 18 | Millwood Goldmine Ruins | 62 | NTC |
| 19 | Belvidere Church | 62 | NTC |
| 20 | Town Walking Tour Knysna | 62 | NTC |
| 21 | Yacht Club Early Landing Sites | 60 | TES |
| 22 | Outeniqua Railroad/Chootjoe | 63 | NTC |
| 23 | Paquila Wreck | 60 | TES |
| 24 | Strandloper Cave 1 | 58 | EH |
| 25 | The Bar & Pilot Station | 62 | NTC |
| 26 | George Rex Grave Site | 62 | NTC |
| 27 | La Fleur Graves | 60 | TES |
| 28 | St Andrew's Church | 60 | TES |
| 29 | Weldon House (orig. Plett Post Office) | 62 | NTC |
| 30 | Athena Wreck | 62 | NTC |
| 31 | Nelson Bay Cave | 58 | EH |
| 32 | Old Whaling Station Site | 63 | NTC |
| 33 | Navigational Beacon | 60 | TES |
| 34 | Old Timber Store Ruins | 60 | TES |
| 35 | Old Rectory | 60 | TES |
| 36 | Van Plettenberg Stone | 61 | TES |
| 37 | St Peter's Church | 60 | TES |
| 38 | Jerling Collection | 60 | TES |
| 39 | Matjies River Rock Shelter | 58 | EH |
| 40 | Forest Hall | 62 | NTC |
| 41 | De Vasselot Camp Site | 62 | NTC |
| 42 | Bloukrans Pass | 60 | TES |
| 43 | Big Tree | 58 | EH |
| 44 | Strandloper Cave 2 | 58 | EH |
| 45 | Storms River Pass | 60 | TES |

*An early navigational instrument (page 132)*

# HISTORICAL INFORMATION

All places of interest are listed and marked on the maps. For further information refer to the following instructions.

| LOCATION | INSTITUTION | TEL. NO. |
|---|---|---|
| Still Bay | Publicity | 028 – 754 2602 |
| Mossel Bay | Bartolomeu Dias Museum | 044 – 691 1067 |
| George | Museum | 044 – 873 5343 |
| Knysna | Angling Club | 044 – 382 4002 |
| Knysna | Library | 044 – 382 5066 |
| Knysna | Millwood Museum | 044 – 382 5066 |
| Plettenberg Bay | Central Library | 044 – 533 2054 |

# ARTS AND CRAFTS

| LOCATION | TEL. NO. |
|---|---|
| Scarab Paper | 044 – 343 2455 |
| Candlepower | 044 – 343 1097 |
| Hot Art | 044 – 343 1123 |
| Bitou-on-the-Water and Bitou Crafts | 044 – 382 3251 |
| Crazy Clay | 044 – 382 5394 |
| The Potter | 044 – 532 7735 |
| The Heath Village | 044 – 532 7724 |
| Jill's Country Collage Antiques | 044 – 532 7740 |
| Elephant Walk Stall | 044 – 532 7833 |
| Weldon Kaya Crafts | 044 – 533 2437 |
| Global Village | 044 – 533 5150 |
| Earth Sea Creations | 082 378 8060 |
| Old Nick Pottery & Weaving | 044 – 533 1395 |
| The Whale Shop | 044 – 533 3743 |
| The Art House | 044 – 533 1673 |
| Porcupine Ceramic Arts | 044 – 534 8910 |
| Langa Lapu | 044 – 534 8827 |
| Knysna Forest Furniture Factory | 044 – 534 8692 |

*The Information Centre at Still Bay is housed in a national monument.*

# GOLF COURSES

Each golf course has its own specific regulations. Please enquire at each club for details.

| LOCATION | TEL. NO. |
|---|---|
| Still Bay Golf Club | 028 – 754 2625 |
| Mossel Bay | 044 – 691 2379 |
| Fancourt | 044 – 804 0000 |
| George Golf Club | 044 – 873 6116 |
| Knysna | 044 – 384 1150 |
| Sparrebosch Golf Club | 044 – 384 1104 |
| Plettenberg Bay Country Club | 044 – 533 2132 |
| Goose Valley | 044 – 533 5082 |

*Fancourt Golf Course in George*

## HORSE AND PONY RIDING

Various stables and riding schools offer day 'outrides' into the wilderness areas and forests, and onto the beaches.

*horse riding
stirrup*

| STABLE | TEL. NO. | RIDES |
|---|---|---|
| Haddows Bridles | 044 – 696 6967 | Various |
| Farmlands/George | 044 – 870 8013 | Pony |
| Forest Horse Rides/Knysna | 044 – 388 4764 | Various |
| Harkerville Horse Rides | 044 – 532 7777 | Various |
| Equatrailing/Plettenberg Bay | 044 – 533 0599 | Various |
| Southern Comfort Horse | | |
| Trails/Plettenberg Bay | 044 – 532 7885 | Various |
| Fourfields Horses (The Crags) | 044 - 53 48708 | Various |

## DRIVING RANGES

| LOCATION | TEL. NO. |
|---|---|
| Mossel Bay | 044 – 691 2379 |
| George | 044 – 871 4001 |
| Plettenberg Bay | 044 – 533 5849 |

*Golf shoes*

## CYCLING

Most of the popular routes have been marked on the map. Some are not designated trails, but are ideal for cycling. Refer to relevant Publicity offices for more information.

| ROUTE | TEL. NO. | DISTANCE | GRADING | Coastal | Forest | Fynbos | Estuary | River | Mountain | AUTH |
|---|---|---|---|---|---|---|---|---|---|---|
| Still Bay Bike Trail | 028 – 754 2602 | Differs | Easy | • | | • | | | | SBM |
| Rein's Coastal Nature Reserve | 028 – 735 3322 | Differs | Easy | • | | • | | • | | P |
| Rein's Coastal Nature Reserve to | | | | | | | | | | |
|   Gourits Mouth | 028 – 735 3322 | 25 km | Varies | • | | | | | | P |
| Geelhoutboom Trail/George | 044 – 801 9295 | 18 km | Easy | | • | | • | | • | GM |
| Outeniqua Adventure Tours/George | | | | | | | | | | |
|   (Little Karoo and Garden Route) | 044 – 871 1470 | 2 – 6 days | Varies | • | • | • | • | • | • | P |
| Montagu Pass Bike Trail/George | 044 – 801 9295 | 12 km | Varies | | • | • | | | • | GM |
| Garden Route Dam/George | 044 – 801 9295 | 3 km | Easy | | • | | | | | GM |
| The Vlei Sand Road/ Wilderness | 044 – 877 0045 | 18 km | Easy | • | | | | | | WT |
| The 7 Passes Rd/Wilderness to Knysna | 044 – 871 4455 | 57 km | Varies | | • | • | | | • | GM |
| Homtini Cycle Route/Knysna | 044 – 382 5466 | 19 km | Varies | | • | | | • | | DWAF |
| Petrus se Brand/Diepwalle | | | | | | | | | | |
|   to Harkerville | 044 – 382 5466 | 24 km | Varies | | • | | | | • | DWAF |
| Harkerville Cycle Routes | 044 – 877 0577 | Differs | Varies | | • | | | | • | DWAF |
| Outeniqua Biking Trails/Plettenberg Bay | 044 – 532 7644 | Differs | Varies | • | • | • | | | • | DWAF |
| Wittedrift Nature Trail/Plettenberg Bay | 044 – 533 4065 | Differs | Easy | | • | | • | | • | PBM |
| Prince Alfred Pass | 044 – 533 4065 | Differs | Varies | | | • | | | • | PBM |
| Robbehoek Cycling Route | 083 261 4826 | Differs | Varies | • | • | • | | | • | P |
| De Vasselot Nature Reserve | 044 – 533 6700 | Differs | Varies | • | • | • | • | • | • | SANP |
| Marine Drive/Bloukrans Forest Station | 042 – 541 1557 | 22 km | Varies | | • | | | | • | DWAF |
| Tsitsikamma National Park/Storms River | 042 – 541 1607 | Differs | Easy | | • | • | | | | SANP |
| Storms River Adventures | 042 - 541 1815 | Differs | Varies | • | • | • | | • | | P |
| Plaatbos Nature Reserve/Storms River | 042 – 541 1815 | Differs | Mod | | • | | | | | DWAF |

# BEACHES

Water temperatures vary from 14° to 23°, depending on seasons and weather conditions. Lifeguards are generally on duty only in December and January, and in the April school holidays.

| LOCATION | Toilets & Showers | Restaurant | Braai facilities | Shop/Kiosk | Lifeguards | Body boarding/Surfing | Tidal Pool | AUTH |
|---|---|---|---|---|---|---|---|---|
| Jongensfontein | • | | • | • | | • | | SBM |
| Shelly | | | | | | | | SBM |
| Lappies Bay | • | • | | • | | • | | SBM |
| Gourits | | | | | | • | | SBM |
| Cannon | | | | | | | | MBP |
| Vleesbaai | | | | | | • | | MBP |
| Santos | • | • | | • | | • | • | MBP |
| Dias | • | | | • | | • | | MBP |
| Hartenbos | • | • | | • | | • | | MBP |
| Little Brak | • | | | • | | • | | MBP |
| Tergniet | • | | | | | | | MBP |
| Great Brak | | | | | | | | GBM |
| Glentana | • | • | • | • | | • | • | GM |
| Herolds Bay | • | • | | • | • | • | | GM |
| Victoria Bay | • | • | • | • | | • | • | GM |
| Wilderness | • | | • | • | | • | | SANP |
| Wilderness Dune | | | | | | • | | SANP |
| Klein Krantz | • | | | | | • | | SANP |
| Swartvlei | • | | | | | • | | SANP |
| Myoli | • | | | | | • | | SM |
| Sedgefield | • | | | • | | • | | SM |
| Goukamma | | | | | | | | WCNCB |
| Buffalo Bay | • | • | • | • | | • | • | WCNCB |
| Brenton | • | • | | • | | • | | KM |
| Coney Glen | • | | | | | • | | KM |
| Knoetzie | | | | | | | | KM |
| Island | | | | | | | | WCNCB |
| Robberg Corner | | | | | | • | | WCNCB |
| Robberg 5 | • | | | • | | • | | PBM |
| Robberg Beacon Island | • | | | | | • | | PBM |
| Central | • | • | • | • | | • | | PBM |
| Hobie | • | | | | | • | | PBM |
| The Wedge | | | | | | • | | PBM |
| Lookout | • | • | | | | • | | PBM |
| Keurbooms | • | | | • | | • | | WCNCB |
| Cathedral Rock | | | | | | | | WCNCB |
| Salt River Mouth | | | | | | | | WCNCB |
| Nature's Valley | • | • | • | • | | • | | SANP |
| Storms River | • | • | • | • | • | • | | SANP |

*Robberg, at Plettenberg Bay is a beautiful beach and a good place to sight whales and dolphins.*

# WHALE WATCHING

Land-based whale watching is at its best from July to October.
See pages 62 - 64 for more information.

| LOCATION | AUTH |
|---|---|
| Die Poort | MBP |
| Fransmanhoek | MBP |
| Gourits Mouth | ABM |
| Great Brak River | GBM |
| Jongensfontein | SBM |
| Lappies Bay | SBM |
| Morris Point | SBM |
| Rein's Coastal Nature Reserve | P |
| Ballots Bay | P |
| Cape Windlass | GM |
| Dolphin Point | GM |
| Herolds Bay | GM |
| Platbank No 1 | WCNCB |
| The Waves B&B | P |
| Wilderness Dune Beach | GM |
| Brenton-on-Sea | P |
| Knoetzie | KM |
| Kranshoek Viewsite | P |
| The Heads | KM |
| Walker Point | SANP |
| Keurbooms Hill | P |
| Nature's Valley | SANP |
| Robberg Nature Reserve | WCNCB |
| Signal Hill | PBM |
| Storms River Mouth | SANP |

*The entries on the grids appear in order of their geographical position on the map, reading from left to right.*

*Southern Right Whale (page 62), the most commonly sighted whales off the Garden Route coast*

# National Sea Rescue Institute

## SEA RESCUE

The NSRI operates all along the Garden Route coast offering emergency life-saving services with their fleet of volunteer-manned Sea Rescue crew. These services required substantial donations.

| LOCATION | EMERGENCY TEL. NO. | |
|---|---|---|
| Mossel Bay | 044 – 10177 | (Metro) |
| | 044 – 691 1911 | (Ambulance service) |
| Wilderness | 044 – 874 2919 | (NSRI) |
| Knysna | 044 – 384 0211 / 384 1078 (NSRI) | |
| | 044 – 302 6600 | (Police) |
| Plettenberg Bay | 10111 | (Flying Squad) |
| | 044 – 533 2744 | (NSRI) |

*Kelp Gulls (page 114), a common sea bird in the area*

*Groot River at Nature's Valley, a peaceful spot to picnic and swim*

## SCUBA DIVING AND SNORKLING

Diving and snorkelling along the Garden Route are excellent. Contact the numbers below for further information, hire of equipment and tuition.

| LOCATION | TEL. NO. |
|---|---|
| Still Bay Diving | 028 – 754 2843 |
| Mossel Bay Diving Academy | 082 896 5649 |
| Beyond the Beach, Plettenberg Bay | 044 – 533 1158 |
| Ocean Safaris, Plettenberg Bay | 044 – 533 4963 |
| Storms River Adventures | 042 – 541 1815 |

*A mask and snorkle enables one to see the underwater environment*

## FRESH WATER SWIMMING

Swimming areas other than in the sea are listed below.

| LOCATION | TEL. NO. | River | Lagoon/Estuary | Municipal Pool | AUTH |
|---|---|---|---|---|---|
| Still Bay | 028 – 754 2602 | • | • | | SBM |
| Little Brak | 044 – 691 2202 | • | • | • | MBM |
| Great Brak | 044 – 620 2100 | • | | • | GBM |
| Wilderness/Island Lake | 044 – 877 0046 | • | • | | SANP |
| Swartvlei | 044 – 877 1197 | | • | • | SANP |
| Groenvlei Lake | 044 – 383 0042 | | • | | WCNCB |
| Goukamma | 044 – 383 0042 | | | | WCNCB |
| Plettenberg Bay | 044 – 533 4065 | | • | | PBM |
| Plettenberg Bay/Keurbooms River and Lagoon | 044 – 533 2125 | • | • | | WCNCB |
| Nature's Valley/Groot River Lagoon | 044 – 531 6835 | | • | | SANP |

*Giant Kingfisher (page 116) is a common freshwater bird .*

*Red Roman*
*(page 71)*

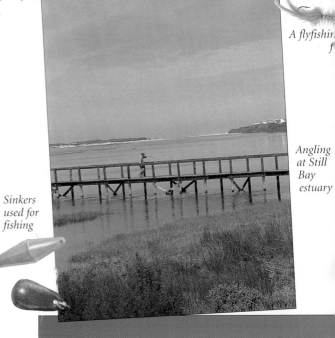

*A flyfishir*
*f*

## ANGLING

Many fish are threatened in the area. Make sure you know the local rules before setting out. See fish species on pages 68 - 73.

*Indicates freshwater angling spots

*Angling at Still Bay estuary*

*Sinkers used for fishing*

| LOCATION | AUTH |
|---|---|
| Voëlklip | SBM |
| Masterstock | SBM |
| Lappies Bay Beach | SBM |
| Preekstoel | SBM |
| Rooibankies | MBM |
| Fransmanshoek | MBM |
| Vleespunt | MBM |
| Pinnacle Point | MBM |
| Die Poort | MBM |
| Romansbank Rocks | MBM |
| Harbour Wall Mossel Bay | MBM |
| Die Bakke | MBM |
| Hartenbos Beach | MBM |
| *Great Brak Estuary/River | GBM |
| Cape Windlass | GM |
| Rooikransies | GM |
| Voëlklip | GM |
| Scotts Bank | GM |
| Preekstoel | GM |
| Jacobs Point | GM |
| Rooiklip | GM |
| Victoria Bay | GM |
| Leentjiesklip | GM |
| Flat Rock | GM |
| Gerickes Point | SANP |
| *Swartvlei Lake/Estuary/Lagoon | SANP |
| Groenvlei | WCNCB |
| Goukamma Beach | WCNCB |
| Platbank No 1 | PBM |
| Goukamma River Mouth | WCNCB |
| Rowwehoek | WCNCB |
| Walker Point | WCNCB |
| Castle Rock | KM |
| *Knysna Lagoon | KM |
| Coney Glen Beach | KM |
| Knoetzie | KM |
| Stevens Bank | PBM |
| Stilbaai | PBM |
| Platbank No 2 | PBM |
| The Island | PBM |
| The Ledge | PBM |
| Kanon Koël Gat | PBM |
| Meide Bank | PBM |
| Beacon Island Rocks | PBM |
| Lookout Rocks | PBM |
| *Keurbooms Lagoon | WCNCB |
| Aventura Eco Plettenberg | P |
| Keurbooms Beach | PBM |
| Picnic Rock | PBM |
| Grootbank | PBM |
| Blue Rocks | PBM |

*Fishing swivels*

## ANGLING CLUBS & INFORMATION CENTRES

All well-known fishing spots are listed and marked on the maps.

| LOCATION | TEL. NO. |
|---|---|
| Still Bay | 028 – 754 2666 |
| Mossel Bay | 044 – 690 7100 |
| George | 044 – 889 0167 |
| George Bass Club (Freshwater) | 044 – 875 9197 |
| Knysna | 044 – 382 4002 |
| Plettenberg Bay | 044 – 535 9740 |

*Fishing rod and hooks*

# Canoeing / Kayaking

| LOCATION | TEL. NO. | HIRE | AUTH |
|---|---|---|---|
| Eden Adventures Garden Route Dam | 044 – 877 0179 | | GM |
| Ebb and Flow/ Wilderness | 044 – 877 1197 | | SANP |
| Fairy Knowe Hotel/Wilderness | 044 – 877 1100 | • | P |
| Eden Adventures/Wilderness | 044 – 877 0179 | | P |
| Lake Pleasant/Sedgefield | 044 – 383 1985 | • | P |
| Groenvlei | 044 – 383 0042 | | WCNCB |
| Goukamma Nature Reserve | 044 – 383 0042 | | WCNCB |
| Dolphin Adventures | 044 – 382 7491 | | P |
| Knysna Eco-Ventures | 044 – 382 5920 | | P |
| Knysna Lagoon | 044 – 382 2905 | | SANP |
| Real Cape Adventures | 082 – 556 2520 | | P |
| Ocean Safaris Plettenberg Bay | 044 – 533 4963 | • | P |
| Aventura Eco Plettenberg Bay | 044 – 535 9309 | | P |
| Keurbooms River | 044 – 533 2125 | • | WCNCB |
| Nature's Valley Lagoon | 044 – 531 6835 | | SANP |

*Sailing boat ropes*

## Sailing

Designated areas have specific regulations. Refer to authorities listed below. Hire and charter vessels and tuition are available.

*Indicates freshwater sailing

| LOCATION | TEL. NO. | AUTH |
|---|---|---|
| Mossel Bay Harbour | 044 – 604 6271 | MBM |
| George / Garden Route Dam (canoes only) | 044 – 801 9295 (Tourism office) | GM |
| *Island Lake/Wilderness | 044 – 877 0046 | SANP |
| *Swartvlei Lake/Sedgefield | 044 – 877 0046 | SANP |
| Baywater Village | 044 – 343 2008 | P |
| *Groenvlei/Sedgefield | 044 – 383 0042 | WCNCB |
| Buffalo Bay/Knysna | 044 – 382 5510 | KM |
| *Knysna Lagoon | 044 – 382 2095 | SANP |
| Springtide Charters/Knysna | 082 470 6022 | P |
| Plettenberg Bay/Hobie Beach | 044 – 533 2941 | PSBC |
| *Nature's Valley Lagoon | 044 – 531 6835 | SANP |
| *Plettenberg Bay/Keurbooms Lagoon | 044 – 533 2125 | WCNCB |

*Mossel Bay harbour, from where one can fish or launch a sail boat*

## Sailing Boat Clubs

| DESIGNATED AREAS | TEL. NO. | AUTH |
|---|---|---|
| Mossel Bay Yacht Club | 044 – 690 7100 | MBM |
| Wilderness | 044 – 877 0053 | SANP |

*Swartvlei Lagoon*

*Spiny Starfish*
*(page 74)*

*Take a boat cruise to Featherbed Reser*
*on the western head of Knysna Hea*

# BOAT CRUISES

*Indicates boats for hire as well

| LOCATION | TEL. NO. | AUTH |
|---|---|---|
| Romana/Mossel Bay | 044 – 690 3101 | P |
| Seven Seas/Mossel Bay | 044 – 691 3371 | P |
| John Benn/Featherbed Reserve Knysna | 044 – 382 1693 | P |
| *Aventura Eco Plettenberg Bay (private except peak time Dec/Jan) | 044 – 535 9309 | P |
| Ocean Adventures/ Plettenberg Bay | 044 – 533 5083 | P |
| Stanley Island/Plettenberg Bay | 044 – 535 9442 | P |
| Dave Rissik | 083 701 3583 | P |
| Storms River Cruises/ Tsitsikamma Nature Reserve | 042 – 541 1815 | P |

*Heart Urchins (page 76)*

# WATER SKIING

This sport is only allowed on water areas listed below.
Please refer to relevant authorities for exact location.

| DESIGNATED AREAS | TEL. NO. | AUTH |
|---|---|---|
| Still Bay | 082 179 2992 | P |
| Great Brak River | 044 – 620 2100 | GBM |
| Sedgefield/ Swartvlei Lagoon/Lake | 044 – 877 0046 | SANP |
| Knysna Lagoon | 044 – 382 2905 | SANP |
| | 044 – 382 5920 | P |
| Plettenberg Bay/ Keurbooms River | 044 – 533 2125 | WCNCB |
| | 044 – 533 3732 | P |

# POWER BOATING

All boating requires permits. Boats may only b
launched from designated launch sites. Ski boa
must remain 300 m away from whales. Refer to
authorities for rules and regulations. *Indicate
freshwater boating.

| LAUNCH SITES | TEL. NO. | AUTH |
|---|---|---|
| Mossel Bay Harbour | 044 – 604 6271 | MBM |
| Great Brak River | 044 – 620 2100 | GBM |
| *Island Lake/Wilderness | 044 – 877 1197 | SANP |
| Sedgefield/ Swartvlei River Mouth | 044 – 877 0046 | SANP |
| Groenvlei Launch Site | 044 – 383 0042 | WCNC |
| *Knysna Lagoon | 044 – 382 2095 | SANP |
| *Lake Brenton Resort | 044 – 381 0060 | P |
| Keurbooms River | 044 – 533 2125 | WCNC |
| Plett Central Beach | 044 – 533 2941 | PSBC |

# SKI BOAT CLUBS

| LOCATION | TEL. NO. | AUTH |
|---|---|---|
| Mossel Bay | 044 – 690 7100 | P |
| Plettenberg Bay | 044 – 533 2941 | PBM |

*The entries on the grids appear in*
*order of their geographical position on*
*the map, reading from left to right.*

## PARAGLIDING

| LOCATION | TEL. NO. |
|---|---|
| Cloud Base / Wilderness | 044 – 877 1414 |
| Wings over Wilderness | 082 412 6858 |
| Smile High/Knysna | 082 652 1952 |

## PARASAILING

| COMPANY | TEL. NO. |
|---|---|
| Mossel Bay | 044 – 691 2202 |
| Ocean Safaris Plettenberg Bay | 044 – 533 4963 |

## BUNGEE JUMPING

This sport is managed by Kiwi Extreme. They are a highly trained and professional crew and have two locations on the Garden Route.

| LOCATION | TEL. NO. |
|---|---|
| Gourits River Bridge | 044 – 697 7001<br>65 m high<br>30 km west of Mossel Bay |
| Bloukrans River Bridge | 042 – 281 1458<br>216 m – World's Hightest!<br>40 km east of Plettenberg Bay |

## AIR FLIPS

The following companies can be contacted for flips and trips.

| LOCATION | TEL. NO. |
|---|---|
| Mossel Bay Helicopters | 044 – 691 2407 |
| Cape Flying Services/George | 044 – 876 9217 |
| African Ramble/Plettenberg Bay | 044 – 533 9006 |
| Ocean Safaris/Plettenberg Bay | 044 – 533 4963 |
| Stanley Island/Plettenberg Bay | 044 – 535 9442 |

*uropean Swallows
nd White-rumped
wifts in flight*

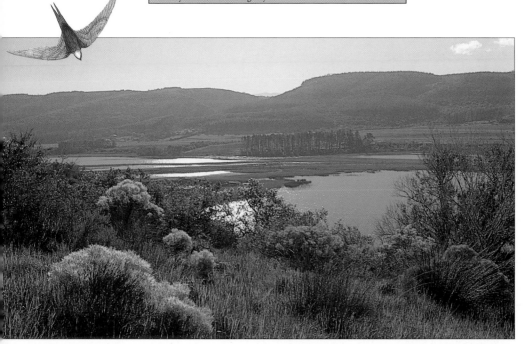

*Many inland areas are ideal for water recreation.*

# LAND AND SEA

The "Garden Route" is a
marketing concept to promote
the beauty of this fragile narrow
strip of extraordinary coastline from
Still Bay to Storms River. The area is
a microcosm of any of the Earth's
major coastal areas – sea shore,
dunes, cliffs, rivers, gorges, estuaries,
lakes and mountains.

The rock layers of the Earth's crust
change with time. Mountain peaks
and river gorges are formed by
weathering and erosion, while
landforms, such as dunes, are the
result of sedimentation.

1. Weathering – This happens
   when rock is broken down into
   smaller pieces by ice, water, heat,
   rivers, glaciers, surf, the effect of
   plant roots and chemical
   reactions.

2. Rock formation – The sediment
   is subjected to millions of years
   of cementing, pressure, heat, and
   often crustal upheaval. This
   gradually forms new rock with
   new characteristics.

3. Erosion – When weathered
   material is transported by water,
   wind, river, waves, ice or gravity,
   this process is called erosion.

4. Sedimentation – Eroded
   material is eventually deposited,
   as sediments, often in layers, in a
   new place.

*A peaceful gorge-side along the Otter Trail
showing Table Mountain quartzite.*

28

# SETTING THE SCENE

The Garden Route landscape is made up of mountain peaks, valleys, dunes, estuaries and other landforms. These are the end-result of a variety of geological processes. Both the landforms, and the processes that form them, are fascinating to understand and to see. The landscape may appear to be fixed, but it is changing all the time. Usually the changes are too small for us to notice, even over a period of decades.

*Close up of quartzite rock showing weathering from ro to sar*

### Earth Structure
The Earth is a sphere with a red hot metallic core, surrounded by a mantle of very hot, soft and supple rock. We live on the very thin, cool crust of the surface.

### Crustal Plates
The crust is made up of many different-sized plates which are floating on the very hot mantle. They move very slowly, up to 15 cm per year. There are eight larger plates shown here. When two plates collide, their edges crumple and fold, and this has monumental implications.

This is how continents are created, or split apart, how mountains are bulldozed upwards, and how vast new oceans flood in between two landmasses. These plates are still moving, and the world map as we know it today will be noticeably different in a million years time.

*If the earth w the size of an app the crust would thinner than apple's sk*

Earth Structure
1. Metallic core
2. Very hot mantle
3. Thin crust

*Quartz pebbles*

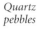

Crustal Plates
1. Pacific Plate
2. Nazca Plate
3. North American Plate
4. South American Plate
5. African Plate
6. Asian Plate
7. Antarctic Plate
8. Indo-Australian Plate

## Gondwana super-continent 400 million years ago (Ma)

Every few hundred million years some of the crustal plates collide and form super-continents. About 400 million years ago (Ma), the area we call the Garden Route, lay under an inland sea on the giant super-continent Gondwana.

Sediment was washed into this sea by rivers flowing from present-day Namaqualand. This was deposited in layers on a granite base. The sediment was pressurised, heated and turned into very hard rock – Table Mountain quartzite (TMQ).

This is distinguished by cracks, faults and weaknesses between layers of the ancient sediments. Many of these intersect each other at acute angles, or close to 90°. To this day these faults and the cracks are visible (map page 30).

Ancient Namaqualand and rivers

Ancient inland sea

Sediments deposited in the sea by rivers

*Earth's mantle*

Ancient granite – part of the Earth's first crust

## The Rise of the Cape Fold Belt Mountains
### (260 - 230 Ma)

Cape Fold Belt Mountains

*The Garden Route shares major features with the southern Cape – the Indian Ocean coastline to the south, and the Cape Fold Belt Mountains to the north.*

About 260 Ma, crustal plate collision led to the final formation of Gondwana. The huge pressure folded, crumpled and tilted the horizontal layers of the sediment and rock, and pushed them upwards. This created a mighty mountain range, thousands of metres high called the Cape Fold Belt Mountains. These mountains include the Outeniquas and the Tsitsikammas.

*Quartz pebbles*

*Pressure*            *Pressure*

Folded layers of sediment

Granite

Mantle

**Upward lift from lateral pressure**

*Pinch the skin on the back of your hand to see this effect.*

*Erosion along many rivers reveals the layers and folding of Table Mountain quartzite.*

# SETTING THE SCENE

## COASTLINE AND SEA LEVEL CHANGES

Of all the planets in our Solar System, Earth is the only one with water and coastlines. The fascinating line where sea meets land is surprisingly unstable. Any major change to the Earth's crust, or to the amount of water in the oceans, profoundly affects the position and shape of coastlines. This in turn alters erosion, sedimentation, rock formation and weather cycles.

*Beach stones sculptured by time and the elements, reveal their intriguing shapes and patter*

### The Indian Ocean Coastline forms (Cretaceous Period – 140 Ma)

About 140 Ma, during the Cretaceous Period, Gondwana was pulled apart by huge movements of the crust. It broke up into several large plates which now form Africa, South America, Australia, India and Antarctica. As Africa and South America separated, the Indian Ocean came into being. This brand new coastline was the start of the Garden Route landscape as we see it today. Both before and after these events, sea level changed many times (see opposite). During times of higher water-level than today, rivers washed sand and mud into the Cretaceous bays around Plettenberg Bay, Knysna and Mossel Bay.

*Indian Ocean forming*

*Sand-eroded rock*

These Cretaceous mud and sand sediments settled, but were never pressurised and heated to the same extent as the TMQ. The resulting Cretaceous mudstone and sandstone are not nearly as tough, and they weather relatively easily. They do not show the acute 90° angle cracks that characterise TMQ.

### Simplified Geology

Mostly sand / sandstone / limestone / fossil dune sand deposited 15 Ma and younge

Cretaceous mudstone deposited about 120 Ma

Table Mountain quartzite (TMQ) deposited about 450 Ma, folded about 260 Ma

George granite deposited about 620 Ma

All the above have associated rocks. For simplicity these have not been included.

*Beach sand – eroded rock and shells*

Changes in global sea level from 140 Ma to the present

~ Fluctuations in sea level    ~ Rivers cut the gorges
— Cretaceous Period    — Tertiary Period    * Present Day

## Sea Level Changes (140 Ma to present time)

During the last 140 million years, the global sea level rose and fell many times, all over Earth. It rose to as high as 300 metres above present level, and as low as 200 metres below. This profoundly affected the Garden Route which was a near-coastal zone during all this time.

Archeological evidence at Nelson Bay Cave at Robberg is clearly displayed for visitors. This cave was used by hunter-gatherers and herders some 18 000 years ago as a shelter (see site 31 on pages 9 & 10). Layers of their domestic refuse (middens) show that their diet changed from sea products, like shellfish, to land animal sources only, and then back to fish again.

*Proof of sea level changes are aided by early humans' utilisation of sea food such as these shells, found in middens (page 130).*

These diet changes occurred because the sea level fell by some 100 metres, and the shoreline receded to a point many kilometres away from the cave. At this time their diet was predominantly meat, because they could not walk to the sea and back in one day. Significant sea level changes are therefore not unusual, and more changes can be expected. Present changes in global climate indicate that a rise in sea level of up to one metre in the next 100 years is likely. If this should happen, the coast would move inland as much as 4 - 5 kilometres in some low-lying areas. Estuaries such as the Keurbooms, Piesang, Knysna (to right) and Kaffirkuils would certainly be flooded. At 300 metres higher, the sea would flow over all the bridges of the gorges and over the entire town of George, right up the Gourits, Piesang, Knysna and Keurbooms River valleys. Olifantsberg (357 m), Vasvoëlberg (354 m) and Spioenkop (340 m) would become islands.

*Areas around Knysna estuary would be flooded with a sea level rise of 1 metre*

### Sea Levels

— Ancient high sea level, often along the mountains

— Present coastline

— Low cretaceous coastline

# WONDERS OF THE SEA

The coastline and its inhabitants are affected by the ocean's currents, waves, winds and climate. The processes that shaped the coast as we see it today, took millions of years, and still continue to alter it.

The daily, weekly, and monthly levels of the sea change with tides. These are the result of the combined gravitational pull of the Sun and the Moon acting on the water of the Earth's oceans. The tide inside an estuary is always later than the tide in the open sea, in the same area. This is because the restriction of the inlet slows down the changes in water level.

*Early inhabitants of the Garden Route (page 130) utilised the tides by building fish traps, which local people still use today. As the tide recedes fish are trapped within the man-made walls, and the people simply collect their meal of fish*

 **Tides**
There are basically two types of tides which alternate through the month – Spring and Neap tides.

### Spring tides
Spring tides occur at full and new moon, at which times the Sun, Moon and Earth lie in a straight line. The water that lies along this line is pulled up higher because of the combined forces. The levels of water of oceans not on this line, are therefore correspondingly lower. Thus at any one time, some of the world's tides are particularly high, and others are particularly low.

### Neap tides
Neap tides occur when the Sun, Earth and Moon form a 90° angle. This happens when the Moon is in the first and last quarters. At this time the pull on the water in the oceans is more evenly distributed around the Earth. Thus there is less difference between high and low tide levels, all around the world.

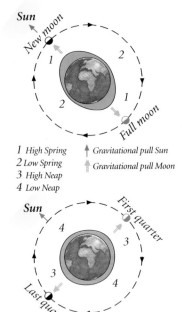

*1 High Spring*
*2 Low Spring*
*3 High Neap*
*4 Low Neap*

↑ *Gravitational pull Sun*
↑ *Gravitational pull Moon*

*Rocks near Mossel Bay exposed at low spring tid*

*Mussel beds (page 78) a exposed at low tid Collectors' note: ea person is allowed a limit quo*

## Average Tide Table

*This summarised tide table for the Garden Route will help you see the correlation between Moon and tides. The tides are shown for the day on which the Moon is new, first quarter, full or last quarter. The tide then moves on average about an hour later each day.*

| | | Time | 08:00 | 09:00 | 10:00 | 11:00 | 12:00 | 13:00 | 14:00 | 15:00 | 16:00 | 17:00 | 18:00 hrs |
|---|---|---|---|---|---|---|---|---|---|---|---|---|---|
| ◐ | *New moon* | Spring | | | | | | | | | | | |
| ◑ | *First quarter* | Neap | | | | | | | | | | | |
| ◑ | *Full moon* | Spring | | | | | | | | | | | |
| ◗ | *Last quarter* | Neap | | | | | | | | | | | |

Low tides ▦    High tides ▰

The relationship between ocean and estuarine tides is seen particularly well in the Keurbooms and Knysna estuaries. The Garden Route's tidal range is called micro-tidal, because there is generally less than 2 metre difference in the water-line between spring high and spring low tides. This controls the type of estuaries and beaches that can form.

*False Plum Anenomes (page 75) have adapted to survive in the ever-changing intertidal zone.*

*In the Southern Hemisphere, as seen from Earth, a **C** moon ◖ is a **C**limbing, waxing moon, and a **D** moon ◗ is a **D**eclining, waning moon.*

*People are often fascinated to see that wherever they are the light of the Moon travels directly towards them over water.*

## Freak Waves

Freak waves can occur anywhere, at any tide, at any time of the year, and have a devastating effect on anything in their path. At any one time and place there may be a number of simultaneous, but different, swell-patterns. Sometimes two or more swell-crests happen to coincide. The resultant wave's height will be the sum of the coinciding, individual wave heights.

In the Garden Route, where there are usually moderate 2 metre swells, there could suddenly be a 4 metre or even 6 metre wave. These short-lived, unusually high swells can become 'freak waves'. Be aware! A freak wave can occur at any place where there is deep water near to the shoreline, e.g. at the foot of a sea-cliff, or on the rocks at the sea's edge. There are a number of places along the Garden Route where freak waves have claimed lives or caused serious injury. They occur at Mossel Bay, Herolds Bay, Victoria Bay, the Knysna Heads, Robberg and along the Otter Trail on the Tsitsikamma coast. When a freak wave breaks, it can flood the adjacent shoreline or rocks and wash away the unwary. There is no warning. The wave rises out of the sea, surges forwards, breaks and is gone.

*Plum Anenome (page 75) is also an intertidal creature.*

Beach
pebbles that have
been rounded
smooth by sea action

# WONDERS OF THE SEA

## THE POWER OF WAVES

Most people presume that a swell is a moving wall of water. This is not true. An ocean swell is the transport of energy: movement of actual water, sand and pebbles only occurs near the shore itself.

### Wind … to Swells … to Waves

A storm transfers energy from the blowing wind to the water, creating swells. These move along the surface of the ocean for hundreds to thousands of kilometres. In shallow water the swell rapidly changes to a wave, and moves stones and sand along the beach. Thus initial storm energy is transferred into erosion that carves a shoreline.

**1**
*Deep sea-swells*

**2**
*Shallower water waves*

**3**
*Surf*

**4**
*Swe*

*Seafloor*

*The formation of wav*

*Seafloor*

### 1. Deep Sea

A swell moves energy in the open ocean. The mass of water through which it travels remains in virtually the same place. Swells only appear to be moving – what we see is energy moving through the water. The passage of this energy causes the water particles to move in circles. They travel up the approaching swell's slope, slightly along the crest, down the swell's receding slope and back to the starting point, in the trough. Below the surface, this circular movement rapidly reduces to nothing. As a result the effect of the swell here is only felt on, and near, the surface. The deep seafloor is not affected by passing swells.

*Water particles moving in a circle due to swell energy*

*A floating bird or boat will show how lit the water moves. In deep water th remain bobbing up the crests and dov the troughs of swells. A human swimmir or on a surf-board, will do the san*

*The slow moving Southern Right Whale out in th deep sea*

## 2. Shallow Water

When an ocean swell enters shallow coastal waters, it loses some of its energy by dragging against the seafloor. This slows the lower portion. The upper portion, however, continues to move. This pushes a wave-crest upwards, steadily higher, as it rushes into shallower and shallower water. The wave increasingly transfers energy to the seafloor, and sand and pebbles are moved.

*Swells entering shallow water at Plettenberg Bay form regular waves in the surf-zone.*

*Surf smashing on the rocks near Storms River*

## 3. Surf-zone

When the water is only a few metres deep, the wave-crest over-balances, crashes down, and a wall of turbulent, moving water surges towards the beach. Here the final swell-energy is used up, and a great deal of erosion and movement of sand and stones takes place. Eventually the thousands of waves that break on the shore every day, carrying abrasive particles in the water, erode the shore to a smooth, wave-cut platform, or to a sea-cliff, or to a bay.

## 4. Swash-zone

The swash rushing up and down a sandy beach sorts the sand grains to a uniform size, and smooths the beach to a flat, even surface.

*The wave's last energy is used up as swash.*

# WONDERS OF THE SEA

## CURRENTS AND WAVES

The Garden Route is a transitional area. It is influenced by both the cold Benguela and the warm Agulhas currents. Most of South Africa has summer rainfall, and the south-western Cape has winter rain. The Garden Route has both.

Slow-flowing cold Benguela Current

Fast-flowing warm Agulhas Current

*Currents that occur along the southern Africa coastline. The Garden Route is affected by both.*

*Red Roman (page 71) are endemic to the warmer Agulhas current coastline.*

### Benguela Current

The Benguela Current flows north from the Antarctic up the west coast of South Africa. The water is cold and therefore the air is dry.
Rain is unusual in the south-west Cape in the summer, and occurs with the onset of cold, wet conditions, associated with the powerful cold fronts of winter.

### Agulhas Current

The Agulhas Current flows south from the equator, bringing warmth, moisture and summer rain from the tropics. By the time the Agulhas reaches the Garden Route, it is flowing east to west. Summer rainfall decrease because the current loses heat as it moves west.

### Garden Route Climate

The Garden Route is also a transitional rainfall area. It is here that the winter rainfall pattern, (from Mossel Bay westwards), changes to summer rainfall experienced in Port Elizabeth northwards. The area can experience strong south-westerly winds throughout the year. These are the main dune-forming winds of the region (see pages 44 - 47). During summer, easterly and south-easterly winds can raise high waves in the east-facing bays. This results in significant erosion of sandy beaches (see pages 42 - 43).

*Doublesash Butterflyfish (page 71) occur in the southern African waters affected by both the Benguela and Agulhas currents.*

*During stormy weather the Mossel Bay Lighthouse warns ships of the rocky coastline.*

*The pattern of swell-sets that arrives at the coastline can be most complex, and a simple pattern is rare.*

## Wave Patterns

Storms in the Antarctic Ocean produce enormous sets of swells. They sweep across the open ocean from the south-west, travelling for thousands of kilometres. In their death-throes they finally disperse their energy as surf, pounding the Garden Route coastline. This has been the pattern ever since the Indian Ocean was first fully developed (page 30). Near the coast, local, easterly storms can create quite large, but short-lived, swell-sets. The size of swells depends on how hard the wind blew, for how long, over what surface area of water, and over what depth. This south-westerly pattern has helped to form many distinctive features of this coastline. In particular read about wave-cut platforms and fossil cliffs (page 38), half-heart bays (page 40 - 41) and dunes (pages 44 - 47).

*Furry-ridged Triton (page 81)*

*Swells breaking onto a flat sandy beach*

*The energies of the currents and waves wash up many shells and other interesting treasures along the high water mark (pages 78, 79). For example the Mermaid's Purse (left) and the Pink-rayed Limpet (right).*

### Swell Direction

*The prevailing wind is from the south-west. In addition the most common swell-pattern from the Antarctic is also from the same direction.*

Still Bay · Vleesbaai · Gouritsmond · Mossel Bay · George · Wilderness · Sedgefield · Knysna · Buffelsbaai · Plettenberg Bay · Nature's Valley · Storms River

N W E S

# WONDERS OF THE COASTLINE

The Garden Route is one of South Africa's most beautiful recreational areas – and it is only due to a unique coastal platform that this is so.

From Mossel Bay to Storms River, this idyllic platform lies between high mountains to the north, and the sea to the south, offering a vast array of opportunities for leisure and entertainment. Understanding how it was formed is fascinating.

### The Wave-cut Platform and Cliffs

As the sea level rises, it moves the abrasive surf-zone 'inland', and when it falls, the surf-zone moves further away. This see-saw changes the coastline continually (page 31).

1. Over many millions of years sea level was repeatedly as much as 300 metres higher than now. For a long time the shoreline was at the foot of the Outeniqua and Tsitsikamma mountains.

2. Later, over millions of years, the sea repeatedly fell and rose again. Each time it fell it revealed a wave-cut seafloor, bounded by steep cliffs where the shoreline had been. Cliffs form along the shoreline when the vertical jointed, hard, Table Mountain quartzite (TMQ) blocks are undercut by the surf. The eroded blocks fall into the sea, leaving a very steep cliff face.

3. At the present position of sea level, we can enjoy the benefits of living on a remarkably flat, coastal platform. The slope of the platform is on average 1:300 seaward, and it varies in width from about 2 km to 30 km.

*Hikers negotiating the sheer rock face, eroded by the power of water.*

(M

Southe.
Rock Agan
(page 11

*Wave-cut platform*

## Sandy Beaches

Where the seafloor has a gentle, even, offshore slope, the waves tend to form a wide surf-zone. The waves start to break some distance away and each surf-wall keeps on rolling in, shedding energy all the way to the beach itself. This is a common scene on sandy beaches such as Hartenbos, Glentana, Sedgefield, Noukamma and Plettenberg Bay. Sandy beaches may develop offshore sand-bars during seasonal changes.

The sandy beach at Great Brak River is a source of sand for the dunes.

This occurs when beach sand is moved offshore rather than along the shore. An offshore sand-bar can be recognised by a double surf-zone. The first surf-zone forms where the larger waves break over the sand-bar. This surf then reforms into swells that eventually break again as a second surf-zone closer to the beach itself. Offshore sand-bars commonly develop off the sandy beaches listed above.

## Rocky Beaches

Where the seafloor slopes steeply, the swells come close inshore, then break suddenly. In extreme cases, for example at a sea-cliff, the breaking water is bounced off the cliff-face and actually pushes off to sea, causing great interference with the incoming swells. This can be seen off the Tsitsikamma coast. These beaches can be dangerous because of the up-rushing surf and the powerful return flow.

African Black Oystercatchers (page 114) nest on sandy or rocky beaches.

## Modern Cliffs

The abrasive surf is a most efficient tool for etching the shoreline shape, depending on the nature of the rock.The straight shoreline of the Tsitsikamma coastline, and the steeply vertical cliffs, are a direct consequence of the very hard, layered and faulted nature of the Table Mountain quartzite (TMQ) in the area.

Abrasive surf at Storms River

Modern sea-cliffs to the west of Marine Drive overlooking the Otter Trail

# WONDERS OF THE COASTLINE

## CREATIVE WATER EROSION

Water itself has no cutting power. As it moves, however, it picks up particles of sand, or pieces of rock, and these have the power to abrade surfaces. Particles in suspension in the waves act on the coastline and create wave-cut platforms, or cliffs. This is similar to imagining that sandpaper only has an effect because of the sand!

**Refraction**

← *Direction of swells refracting around the headland*
― *Sandy beach in half-heart bay*

*Pink-lipped Topshell (page 78)*

### Refraction

It is easier to understand refraction once you have read how swell-energy is lost in shallow water, as the swell drags on the seafloor (see pages 34 - 35). When a swell-system approaches the coast at an angle, that part of the swell that meets the shallower coast first, slows down. This slower moving section does not travel forwards with the rest of the swell, but deflects, or 'refracts', until it eventually becomes a wave parallel with the shore. At a headland the swell breaks as a wave, and curls around the obstruction. The remainder of the swell continues forward, in its original direction, at the same speed. All along the curve of a bay, the end of the swell travelling in the shallow water refracts on the seafloor and curls around until the waves approach the shore parallel to a beach.

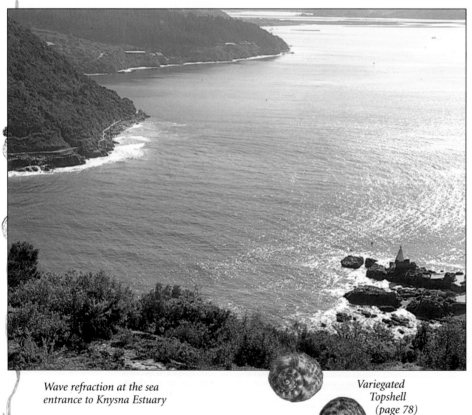

*Wave refraction at the sea entrance to Knysna Estuary*

*Variegated Topshell (page 78)*

*Looking south-west over Buffelsbaai – a classic half-heart bay*

## Half-heart (Log-spiral) Bays

1. The ancient Garden Route coastline consisted of alternating areas of harder TMQ and softer Cretaceous mudstone and sandstone (see pages 30 - 31). As the newly formed Indian Ocean changed to its present shape, the sea swells increasingly approached from the south-west.

*Venus Ear (page 80)*

2. Over millennia, countless waves beat against the shore, eroding it slowly but surely. The resistant TMQ remained as headlands, and the Cretaceous mudstone and sandstone formed bays.

3. As the waves refracted around the headlands, the bays were deeply eroded into the distinctive half-heart shape we see today. The bays are sculpted on the northern side of the headlands.

| | |
|---|---|
| Sea | Cretaceous mudstone & sandstone |
| Table Mountain quartzite | Swell direction |
| | Half-heart bays |

*The half-heart shape of bays formed by refracted swells are a precise mathematical curve called a logarithmic spiral – thus a 'log-spiral' bay. This is a similar mathematical spiral that is seen in whirlwinds, whirlpools, pinecones, spiral galaxies, and in sea shells (see examples on these pages, and Ram's Horn Shell on right).*

### Coastline Features

- Half-heart bays
- Fossil cliffs
- Wave-cut platform

# Wonders of the Coastline

## Beaches and Currents

Coastal features are created through the interaction of waves, local coast-hugging currents and tides. Beaches offer superb opportunities for recreation, and understanding the processes can certainly increase your fun and your safety too.

Refer to grid page 20 for information on the different beaches.

*Along the beach the movement of sand continues in a zigzag pattern between each up and down swash. The longshore current nudges the sand grains, or other floating matter, in one direction, down-current, all the time.*

Headland

← *Swash* ← *Approaching wave*
← *Wave-swell direction*

### Longshore Drift

Close inshore, in the surf-zone, the longshore current moves sand from beach to beach, continuously, like a natural conveyor belt. The longshore current is particularly effective where wave refraction is well developed, like around headlands. The turbulence of the breaking surf here helps to keep sand grains in suspension so that the longshore current can move them (see Refraction, page 40).

1. The concentrated surf at a headland lifts sand into suspension and provides energy for transport.

2. This energy from the refraction at the headland drives the current strongly into the bay.

3. The current weakens in the bay, and its load of sand is dropped to form a sandy beach.

A longshore drift may be responsible for the erosion of large quantities of beach sand. Along the Garden Route it can move more than a hundred thousand cubic metres of sand past a given point per year. That represents a pile of sand 50 m long, 50 m wide and some 40 m high! Swimmers are often well aware of the longshore drift. On these occasions when they find themselves drifting down the shoreline, away from the point where they entered the water, they can assume the swell-energy at the nearby headland is particularly strong.

*Horn-eyed Ghost Crab (page 78) c be seen mo sidewards along the shoreline.*

*A longshore drift moves sand along bays like at Gerickes Point, Sedgefield.*

*Sandy tombolo linking Robberg and The Island on the right*

## Tombolos

Where a sandy beach connects an island to the mainland, a tombolo is created. Its distinctive hourglass outline is the result of waves refracting around both sides of an island onto the tombolo beach. There are very few tombolos in South Africa. Possibly the best example is the beach at The Island on the south side of Robberg. Here refraction causes the surf to curl around both sides of the Island. At the tombolo beach, waves actually approach each other from opposite sides. The resulting double curvature of the tombolo shows a half-heart and its mirror image, which is very rare. These beaches are the mathematical curves of two sets of refracted waves.

*A Brown Mussel shell (pages 75, 78), filled with sand*

← *Swell direction*

← *Rip current*

## Rip Currents

From time to time, sandbars and gulleys form on the seafloor where there are breakers. The breaking waves can drive excess water close to the beach, and here, momentarily, the water is trapped. The piled-up water quickly rushes back out to sea along a gulley, much faster that the normal backwash that tugs at a wader's legs. The stream lasts only a very short while and dissipates just seaward of the surf-zone. This is a rip current, and is responsible for many drownings when unwary swimmers get swept out to sea and panic. The secret is to relax, to wait for the rip current to stop, and then to float back with the incoming waves. Rip currents also develop in rocky areas. Where there is a gulley between two rocks that are low enough for a wave to break over them, and a small bay on the shore side, water can again be trapped. The pull of the receding surf causes a similar, dangerous rip current.

*A typical rocky shore where rip currents occur*

# ALL ABOUT DUNES

The dunes and lakes (pages 48 - 49) that form the landscape of the Wilderness are inextricably linked in their origin. The dunes are the fascinating result of sea level changes (see pages 30 - 33), whereas the lakes formed in the inter-dune valleys as the sea retreated.

Ancient dune-fields were formed repeatedly along this coast in the past. Some large ones were fossilised and are still visible today. Active dunes also occur, but they are generally small.

## Dunes and Dune-fields

Wind action forms dunes which may range in size from less than a metre to two hundred metres high. Several kinds of dunes can form depending on wind speed, consistency of the wind, grain size, climate, presence of plants, and other conditions. Dunes and dune-fields commonly form along the coast where onshore winds blow across a sandy beach, sweeping sand inland. To move sand away, wind has to blow at a speed of at least 5 metres per second, which is 18 km/h (9,7 knots).

*Cape Dune Molerat (page 102)*

The systematic downwind transport of sand, shown below, has the effect of moving the entire dune downwind. In the Garden Route area, small, coastal dunes usually move downwind at a rate of about 4 to 10 metres per year.

*Christmas Berry (page 99) grows on coastal dunes*

*New and developing dunes*

1. Any obstruction, like a plant, stone, rock, log, or even a house, which causes the wind to slow down, will cause air-borne sand to be deposited. This could be the start of a dune which, as it grows, will generate its own further growth, by slowing the wind.

2. As the dune grows, the sand is swept up the slightly convex, windward face.

3. The grains are blown beyond the crest, and once there are drawn into the turbulence which forms in the lee of the dune. Here the speed drops, the wind can no longer keep the sand in suspension, and it is deposited on the lee slope (called the slipface).

*Sea Pumpkin (page 98)*

*Dunes forming around various plant species*

### Wind Action lifting Sand – Saltation

Wind-blown sand is transported in a cloud of bounding, jumping grains close to the surface. Grains are in turn lifted, carried a distance, which is dependent on the wind speed, then dropped. As they hit the surface, they knock a number of other grains into the air. This spray of airborne grains is carried further along by the wind.

Anyone who has been on a sandy beach during a gale has felt the sting of the sand grains on their legs. This specific wind-sand action is called saltation.

*Wind action lifting sand*

*Dunes forming the back-drop to Robberg Beach, Plettenberg Bay*

# ALL ABOUT DUNES

## ACTIVE AND FOSSEL DUNES

The dunes and lakes are among the youngest of the landscape features along the Garden Route, being no more than 2 million years old. Dunes occur at those areas where sufficiently strong local winds can blow beach sand inland.

Active dunes

Fossil land dunes

Fossil drowned dunes

*Sea Lavender*
*(page 98)*

 **Active Dunes**
### The Climbing-falling Dune of Robberg

On the northern side of Robberg, is Witsand, an unusual dune, which is a clear white landmark. All year round the south-westerlies blow the sand up the southern slopes of Robberg from the tombolo beach at The Island. At the top the sand drops down the precipitous cliff onto a narrow beach or straight into the surf, 50 metres below. The powerful wind lifts many, many tons of sand every year up the full height of Robberg.

*Pig's Ear*
*(page 98)*

*Witsand - the "falling" dune of Roberg*

At Witsand itself, the dune slipface shows quite dramatically the characteristic 34° slope of all dunes. Here the sand that accumulates in the wind-shadow behind the crest, slides down the steep surface, under the influence of gravity. This area is unstable and can slump at any time. Do not walk on the slipface.

## Fossil Dunes

The orientation and size of fossil dunes of the Garden Route prove that for the past 15 million years south-westerlies have been the most common winds. Among the largest of the fossil dune-fields is the one at Wilderness, which was formed during the Pleistocene, some 2 million years ago. They are easily recognised as dunes by their shape, even though they are now fully covered in vegetation.

Dune-sand along the coast commonly contains a lot of shell fragments amongst the quartz sand grains. Rain water seeping through the dune dissolves some of the shell pieces and, when a dune is left undisturbed for a long enough period, this cements the sand grains together. The resultant hard mound of rock that is created is a fossil dune, that can survive for millions of years in the same place. Robberg, and particularly The Island, are among the places where the grainy, abrasive, easily eroded rocks that make up a fossil dune, are easy to see.

*Sour Fig*
*(page 98)*

## Fossil Drowned Dunes

When sea level was lower, dune-fields developed on the then exposed seafloor, well beyond our present coastline. Over millennia they fossilised, and were later flooded and submerged by the rising sea. These dune-fields still exist, 2 - 7 km offshore, and can be traced with echo-sounding equipment on boats.

The best known section is a reef about 3,5 km offshore, 12 km long and about 2 km wide, which lies between Sedgefield and Buffelsbaai. Its crest is about 10 metres below the surface, and is regularly visited by fishermen (see diagram and map).

*The slipface where wind-blown sand is deposited*

## Fossil Land Dunes

Two fossil dune-ridges (cordons), can be recognised clearly as the lines of hills in the Wilderness lake-land. The fossil dunes between Groenvlei and the sea are about 200 metres high from base to top, which makes them the highest in South Africa. The road to Map of Africa, near Wilderness, winds its way up the sea-cliff, and here there are wonderful vantage points for viewing the lakes and dune-ridges. Dolphin Point, on the N2 between George and Wilderness, also offers a spectacular vista to the east.

*Looking towards Spioenkop over Swartvlei*

## Spioenkop

The most inland fossil dunes occur at Spioenkop, shown in the picture above, across Swartvlei Lake. The dunes reach an elevation of almost 350 metres, because they lie on the wave-cut platform, which locally itself has an elevation of about 200 metres above sea level (see diagram below).

*Duine (dune)-aandblom (page 93)*

Modern cliff · Groenvlei dune and lake · Spioenkop · Wave-cut platform · Fossil cliff
400 m
200 m
Fossel drowned dunes
Sea level

*Relationship between dunes, lakes and land*

# LAKES

The Wilderness lake-land is not only scenically beautiful, but also offers wonderful recreational opportunities. The lakes are too small and too shallow to develop any large waves, regardless of wind strength, and are therefore ideal for boating activities like canoeing, kayaking and wind-surfing.

*Grey Herons (page 118) are a common sight around the Lakes in the Garden Route area.*

### The Wilderness Lakes

These were formed by the natural damming of water in the valleys, between two dune-ridges. The lakes are particularly interesting because each has a different working structure. The Knysna and Swartvlei lagoons are open to the sea, and are tidal. They therefore function more like estuaries than true lakes (see page 56). There is a small map on page 55 to show the Lake area.

400 m        400 m

Spioenkop

200 m

Island Lake    Langvlei    Rondevlei    Swartvlei Estuary    Ruigtevlei    200 m

Sea level                               Sea level

*Some of the Garden Route Lakes showing their levels are, on average, consistant with sea level.*

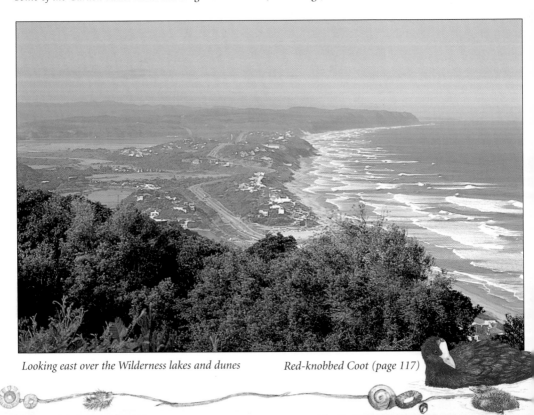

*Looking east over the Wilderness lakes and dunes*     Red-knobbed Coot (page 117)

*Dune Slack Rush (page 99), a sedge that is dominant along the banks of Swartvlei at Sedgefield (hence the name).*

*Swartvlei, a popular recreation area*

*Water Beetle, Family Dytiscidae (20 mm)*
*Water beetles occur in freshwater rivers and lakes, like Groenvlei. They can fly and swim underwater. They use their oar-like back legs to swim, and to trap fresh air in the space between the wings and abdomen. This air acts as a waterlung.*

## Island Lake, Langvlei and Rondevlei

Island Lake is connected to the Touw River Estuary by the Serpentine, a meandering channel that regularly feeds tidal water into and out of its opening. The Touw in flood can back up the Serpentine, raising Island Lake's water level by more than 2 metres in 12 hours or less. A narrow channel connects Island Lake, Langvlei and Rondevlei. Therefore the latter two are also salty. The filling of these lakes is not only via the Touw estuarine water. It is also by underground seepage, possibly even of sea water, through the barrier dunes.

## Groenvlei

Groenvlei is by contrast a completely freshwater lake, which gives rise to the conspicuous reed growth around its shores. Groenvlei's water is only obtained through run-off and seepage from the surrounding dunes. In some maps of the 1940s, it is marked as 'seasonal', indicating its dependence on run-off from nearby dunes when it rains.

*Estuarine Roundherring (page 72) have adapted to freshwater conditions in Groenvlei, which was once connected to the sea.*

*Looking across Groenvlei Lake, from the N2 to the Groenvlei vegetated fossil dunes.*

# RIVER POWER

Rivers, their valleys, gorges, estuaries and river-mouths are dramatic landforms along the Garden Route. The flowing water of rivers significantly influences the landscape. They scour away rocks and soil, and then deposit the sediments further downstream.

Rivers have transformed the local landscape many times before, and will do so again.

## The Power of Rivers

The primary driving force of rivers is, of course, gravity. Rivers do most of their erosive work in their beds. Normally they are not efficient during times when flow is low, or as they get close to sea level. While in flood, however, they grind the bedrock away, and transport their sediment to the sea.

There is indirect erosion on the valley slopes by rain and gravity. Rocks and soil wash and slide into the flowing water below, and widen the valley sides.

Rivers world-wide work towards establishing their own stable river gradient. This has a steeper initial section, flattening out towards the coasts. The slope is dependent on the height the river drops, and the distance to the coast.

*River pebbles, pounded to shape by the power of river water*

*The Twee-riviertjies waterfall, near Storms River, demonstrates the power of wat*

Stable river gradient

Coastline and river mouth

. Along the Garden Route, the upper sections of rivers commonly have narrow valleys and a steep gradient. Here the water flows fast, like in mountain torrents. Rapids and waterfalls are common.

. Downstream the valleys are commonly wider, and the river-flow becomes more sedate. Erosion is therefore more lateral, and the sides of the valleys tend to be much wider.

. At the end of its journey, near the sea, river-flow is slow. Rivers that enter the sea through Table Mountain quartzite (TMQ) tend to form gorges, while those which finish on softer rock tend to form estuaries. At the estuary the direction of river-flow can be reversed temporarily, while the tide comes in.

## Rejuvenation

While a river flows over land which is neither rising nor falling, relative to sea level, it will work to establish a stable river gradient. If, however, the sea level drops, the river 'rejuvenates'. This means that the river regains some of its 'youthful' energy. Its original mouth is now again **above** sea level and therefore needs to reconnect with the sea. It begins working at establishing a second stable river gradient, between its previous mouth, and the new sea level.

Many small rivers along the Tsitsikamma flow entirely on the wave-cut platform. Because they have a small catchment area, and the platform has a low gradient, their present erosive power is limited. They have not yet cut gorges, nor do they have estuaries. All of them, however, have the advantage of entering the sea at the modern sea-cliff, and this will help increase their slope by rejuvenation. It won't be long before they cut their own mini-gorges.

At least one of these little rivers, the Twee-riviertjies, about three hours walk along the beginning of the Otter Trail, is visibly demonstrating its potential vigour, tumbling into the sea by a waterfall (see left). The picture on the right shows a young river, rising on the platform, with enough energy to ultimately cut a mini-gorge (see pages 54 - 55).

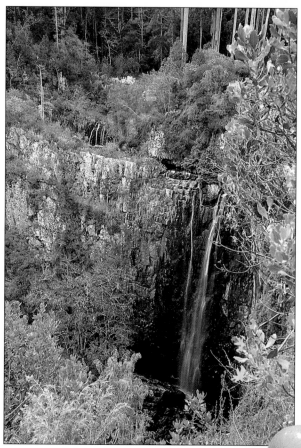

*Brakenhill Falls on the Witels River near Knysna*

Previous mouth    New mouth    — — — Stable river gradient

— — — 2nd stable river gradient

# RIVER POWER

## RIVER PATTERNS

Even the larger rivers along this coast, except the Gourits, rise either in the Tsitsikamma, Outeniqua or Langkloof mountain ranges, or on the wave-cut platform between the ranges and the sea. This means their catchment areas are relatively small. Only the Gourits has the capacity to regularly discharge a large amount of water into the sea. Being very local rivers, that do not pass through heavily industrialised and urban areas, most of the water is unusually clean and unpolluted.

The 'pattern' of the rivers and their tributaries changes according to whether they flow across Table Mountain quartzite (TMQ), granite or Cretaceous mudstone. (see map).

 *The tree-like (dendritic) pattern is typical of rivers that drain Cretaceous mudstone and sandstone areas, as well as the granite area near George.*

### The Gourits River

This is the largest and longest river in the Garden Route, draining from the Oudtshoorn area beyond the watershed of any of the other rivers here. The Gourits River cuts a gorge through the raised floor of a fossil half-heart bay that originally lay west of Mossel Bay, (see page 41). The original TMQ headland that protected the half-heart bay is at the Aasvoëlberg, and the Gourits has cut a gorge even through this obstruction in its way.

### The Rivers of the George Plain

All the rivers of the George plain, including the Little Brak River to the west, are young rivers developed entirely on the wave-cut platform. The George plain lies on granite. This gives rise to the distinctive tree-like drainage pattern seen in most of the rivers drawn on the map above.

### The Piesang River

This small, young river has its own somewhat lopsided gorge. The river flows through a Cretaceous mudstone basin. It has resistant TMQ on the north side of the 'gorge', whereas, the other side of the valley has a gentle slope. This side is mudstone and sandstone, which is unable to maintain the steep slopes characteristic of the TMQ.

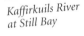 *Kaffirkuils River at Still Bay*

 *The Goutrits River near its estuary*

*TMQ naturally breaks along straight lines and at acute angles (see page 30). This gives the drainage pattern of rivers a square grid-like (trellis-like) appearance.*

*Eastern Cape Redfin Minnow (page 10) is threatened. It is endemic, and found in the Keurbooms river system.*

## e Keurbooms
## er

headwaters of the
rbooms River
e from the
gkloof, north
he main
sikamma
untain range.
s river was already
ving when sea
l was 300 metres
ve its present
l. The placid
ers of its estuary
e the tortuous
rney of the mother stream
ugh the inland mountain valleys. Its gorge is
ctacular and well worth a voyage upstream to enjoy
unspoilt, unpolluted beauty.

*Keurbooms River, near Aventura Eco Plettenberg, peacefully reflects its surroundings*

## e Storms River System

Storms River has a steep, mountain stream
lient over most of its course, that has helped it cut
nagnificent gorge. In addition it happened to strike
nvenient weak zone to use as a bed. Its water flows
rously and turbulently, especially during flood,
n it does most of its erosive work. The near-vertical
walls of the Storms River gorge are a testimony to
hardness of the TMQ, as well as an indication of
power of the river. The other interesting thing to
e is how the main tributary, the Witteklip River,
meets the Storms River at nearly 90°,
because of the pattern
of weak zones in
the TMQ.

e Clawless Otter (page 105)
nd in most pristine river areas

*The upper reaches of Storms River*

# GORGES

All the gorges look more or less alike, and although their depth varies, it is generally around 230 metres.

The very narrow width of a gorge valley, compared with its depth, and the near-vertical layers of Table Mountain quartzite (TMQ) that form the side walls, are spectacular. The numerous cracks and joints in the rock, along which the river excavated its channel, are easy to see in many places.

*Krantz (cliff) Aloe (page 97) grow on the steep slopes of rocky gorges.*

### How the Gorges were made

For a very long time, possibly for more than 50 million years, the local shoreline was at the foot of the Tsitsikamma Mountains. During this time, surf erosion formed a wide, submerged, wave-cut platform. From time to time sea level dropped for a while, exposing the platform to the erosive action of the rivers.

When sea level drops, the natural response of the rejuvenated river is to deepen its valley (see page 51). Valley deepening takes place at a much faster rate than widening of the valley sides. In the very hard Table Mountain quartzite (TMQ), the valley sides remain nearly vertical. The repeated process of sea level drop and rise helped the rivers to cut the gorges to their present depth. The process continues at present, and valley deepening is still more important than widening.

*Cape Chestnut (page 84) grows in river valleys.*

*Active gorge-cutting at the magnificent viewsite, Map of Africa, near Wilderness*

## Gorges made History

Since the earliest humans enjoyed the benefits of the wave-cut platform and its bounty, the gorges have formed a major obstacle to human travel in the region.

*Tree-fuschia (page 88)*

nter-gatherers, and later herders, followed animal paths nake their way down and up the precipitous cliff faces. gorges formed natural barriers that both limited and tected early human endeavour along the coast. When opean settlers arrived, the flat platform was ideal for ning. However, because travel along the coast was ited by the gorges, a harbour was developed at Knysna, pite its hazardous entrance at The Heads. Because of insurmountable engineering problems, a railway nection was never established across the gorges, except r the Gourits.

n the original mountain road passes were a major omplishment. The road makers also tried to follow the jinal elephant paths through the valleys as closely as sible. The first gorge to be bridged was the Storms er (mid-1950s), with the others following during the 1970s.

*Up the Storms River gorge from its mouth*

se single-span concrete arch bridges are among the highest in Africa. They have olutionised road travel along the Garden Route, and afford a spectacular grandstand view of the ges up and down river. But the old roads that wind their way down the narrow valleys, to the om, and up the other side, are equally impressive. Driving these roads will show you how steep and deep the gorges are. You will be aware of the obstacle that they have presented to man and animal alike, for the past hundreds of thousands of years.

*Forest Tree-fern (page 84)*

*The modern bridge over Groot River*

*Khoekhoe herders would have followed animal paths to negotiate gorges.*

### Lakes and Gorges

Gorges

Lake area

*Common Sand Hermi[t] Crab (page 77)*

# RIVERS MEET THE SEA

Near the places where rivers meet the sea we find river mouths and estuaries, and often wetlands. The differences are interesting.

## Estuaries

Estuaries develop where sea water and river water mix in the lower sections of the river during the change of the tides. Estuaries are very important breeding grounds for fish (pages 72 - 73).

## River Mouths

These develop where the river flows directly into the sea. The level of the river-bed is such that, even at high tide, hardly any sea water flows into the river-channel.

## Wetlands

These are marshy areas, either fresh or brackish. They occur along the edges of estuaries and in more inland, low-lying areas, such as river flood-plains.

## Estuaries and Lagoons

The 'mouth' of an estuary is called the 'inlet', a name that stresses the significance of the influence of [t] in-flowing sea water during a rising tide. Along the Garden Route larger estuaries maintain open mouths. However, the small tidal range of the Garden Route co[?] causes many of the smaller estuaries to have a sand-ba[r] across the inlet. These are not always open to the sea.

There are large estuaries with open inlets at Keurbooms-Bitou, Knysna, Swartvlei, Little Brak, Gr[?] Brak and Gourits.

Four estuaries that are closed at time[s] are the Groot, Touw, Piesang and Hartenbos. Closed estuaries create mo[re] of a lagoon than a true estuary. When t[he] end of a river has only a seepage outlet to the sea, through sand blocking the mouth, it is called a lagoon.

*Knysna Seahorse (page 72) is a threatened species that is found in the Knysna estuary.*

*Glasswort Samphire (page 99)*

*The Knysna Estuary is unusual in that it has a fixed rocky inlet, The Heads. In other ways, however, it functions much like estuaries with migrating inlets.*

The Kaaimans River mouth at low tide

## River Mouths

Many of the small rivers along the Tsitsikamma coast flow directly into the sea. The Kaaimans, one of the larger river-mouths, shows a dramatic plume of rusty brown forest water mixing with the white foam of the surf breaking in the mouth. This is particularly impressive during the ebb-tide, when the river-water streams conspicuously into the sea.

Whimbrel
(page 119)

## Wetlands

Wetlands are significant breeding grounds for various organisms, and form buffers for flood-waters. The flood-plain of the Bitou is an excellent example of a wetland. From the vantage point of a local hill slope, the snake-like meandering channels, and U-shaped oxbow lakes and marshes, testify to the changing conditions in the flood-plain. The wetlands of the Touw and Serpentine rivers, at Wilderness, are equally interesting, with the same features.

Black-winged
Stilts (page 119)

The excellent birding area of the Bitou wetlands

# RIVERS MEET THE SEA

## THE KEURBOOMS ESTUARY

Keurbooms is the most beautiful, and the best example of an estuary along this coast. It is easy to access, both along its land and sea shores. It is spectacular to look at, especially from the many vantage points along the Table Mountain quartzite (TMQ) hill on its south-western boundary. It is used here as an example of how estuaries work in general. Follow the numbers 1 - 7 to help you to understand the dynamic system of an estuary.

*Key to Keurbooms Estuary looking nor[th]*

### 1. The Inlet

The appearance of the Keurbooms inlet changes often. Prior to 1915, it was at Lookout rocks, when a major river flood broke through at the northern end of the estuary. However, the new inlet immediately started migration southwards towards Lookout again, at a rate a few metres per year. This is clearly seen in the erosion of the southern inlet bank, and the growth of the northern barrier beach (see 4). It is likely that the process will repeat itself, should the Keurbooms come down again in a major flood.

*Heart Urchins (page 76)*

*iant Kingfisher (page 116) feed n Marsh and Mud Crabs (page 77)*

## 2. The Flood-tidal Delta

At low tide prominent sandbanks are exposed opposite the inlet. Their shape changes all the time, but usually the delta is made up of one or more gracefully curved half-moons of sand. They are formed by seasand that is carried into the estuary by the rising tides – hence the name.

This is an unusual 'delta' because it lies on the landward side of the inlet. Conventional deltas develop on the seaward side. The constantly shifting sand makes it very difficult for burrowing animals to establish themselves and to live here.

## Sub-tidal Channels

*en at low spring tide, the sub-tidal channels remain filled with water. The rush of water leaving the estuary uses turbulence in the inlet. The resultant erosion helps undercut the southern bank of the inlet, aiding its igration southwards.

## The Barrier Beach

its wake the migrating inlet leaves behind a barrier beach, which is a combination of beach and low dunes. e barrier beach is formed by waves and the longshore current (see pages 42 - 43). There is an established plant mmunity on the southern part, but only a few pioneer plants live in the bare sand along the wly formed northern tip of the barrier.

ere are other Barrier Beaches at some of the smaller estuaries, notably the Groot and the uw. These barriers form faster than the rivers can breach them. The estuaries exchange sea water d fresh water by seepage, and are only infrequently, and for a short time, open to the sea.

*Marsh Crab (page 77)*

### 5. Supra-tidal Flats

These flats are raised above normal high tide. A fascinating variety of salt-tolerant plants grow here. They are only covered by sea water during spring tide storms. A myriad of small burrowing crabs make their home here. This is also a superb birding area.

### 6. Inter-tidal Flats

These flats stretch for some distance upstream. Their surface is relatively flat and firm, and is characteristically rippled by the flowing water. They are home to shrimps and pencil-bait that make distinctive burrows in the sand.

### 7. Inter-tidal Lagoon

The south-western end of the estuary is a lagoon with no through-flow. The reed-banks along the shore indicate fresh water springs coming from the TMQ in the cliffs behind the lagoon. These are characterised by muddy sand, lots of estuarine Cape Eelgrass (*Zostera capensis*) and a large population of shells and other invertebrate animals. They burrow so extensively in the sand that anyone walking here sinks knee-deep into the maze of holes and burrows.

### 8. Direction to Lookout Rocks

### 9. Wave-cut Platform

See text on page 38 and map on page 43.

*Sea Pumpkin (page 98) is one of the pioneer plants that stabilises sand.*

# SEA LIFE

There are so many miracles along the Garden Route coast it is no wonder that since the earliest days of hunter-gatherers in southern Africa this has been a mecca for human activity. Part of the appeal has always been the sea life that teams in the ocean itself, as well as along the shore.

The coastline consists of long stretches of sandy beaches interrupted by rocky shores and cliffs. Different zones occur along the beach – the richest zone with the most diversity is the intertidal zone (the area between low and high tide) which is exposed to continual wave action. Here animals thrive in abundance – snails and mussels lie hidden beneath the sand, while diverse invertebrate communities live on the rocks.

Out in the ocean there are a number of zones or habitats. The open water (pelagic region) supports animals like whales, game fish and jellyfish, while the ocean bottom (benthic region) is where creeping animals like Sand Prawns and Sea Urchins live. Rocky reefs can also form out in the deep ocean, on which many different organisms depend for survival.

*Crustaceans and their shells, fish and mammals are all measured in length, unless otherwise stated.*

*This Southern Right Whale could easily be mistaken for a barnacle-covered rock.*

# SEA MAMMALS

Although there is a great diversity of marine mammals occurring off the Garden Route coast (up to 40 species), the ones you are most likely to see are illustrated on these pages. Only one indigenous seal species occurs here, the rest are whales and dolphins. Like other mammals, these animals breathe air, are warm-blooded and give birth to live young, which they suckle. They have a thick layer of fatty blubber for insulation.

## WHALES

Whale hunting has fortunately been banned since 1986, and there are also laws which prevent people from boating within 300 metres of whales. Some whales spend the summer near the Antarctic, feeding on krill (tiny shrimps) before migrating north to warmer waters for the winter.

*For whale watching hotspots see page 20. Take a pair of binoculars and focus beyond and in the breakers to spot whales and dolphins.*

◄ **Humpback Whale** ►
*Megaptera novaeangliae* (15 m)
Humpbacks are named after the small hump on their backs. They often jump out of the water and slap their flukes or flippers as a form of communication, to remove parasites or simply for fun!

They vary in colour and some are completely white. Males sing complex melodies, repeating themes for up to 20 minutes. They are seen from June to November during their migration between their breeding grounds off Mozambique and their feeding grounds in the Antarctic.

**Southern Right Whale** ►
*Eubalaena australis* (14 - 16 m)
These are the most common whales off the southern coast. They were known as the 'right' whales to hunt because they are slow moving and float once killed, so it is easy to bring them back to shore. With hunting now banned, their population is slowly increasing. Barnacles and whale-lice attach themselves onto patches of raised rough skin on the whales' heads. Researchers use these pale-brown patches to identify individual whales. These whales are seen mostly during August and September, when the females calve in sheltered, sandy-bottomed bays. For three months, the calves drink 200 litres of milk a day to build up blubber for the long trip to the Antarctic. The illustration shows a female carrying her calf on her back.

## Comparison of the whales depicted on this page

| Southern Right Whale | Humpback Whale | Bryde's Whale |
|---|---|---|

**Southern Right Whale:** The head has callosities (pale, rough patches of skin); each whale has a different pattern; long, narrow baleen plates.

**Humpback Whale:** The head has golf-ball sized knobs (with sensory hairs) on top of head and lower jaw; baleen is short and wide; head about 1/3 of body length; there are throat grooves.

**Bryde's Whale:** The head has three parallel ridges running from near tip of snout to near blow-hole; baleen is short and wide, and brownish or greyish; there are throat grooves.

**Southern Right Whale:** The tail fluke is very broad – 3,5 m across; smooth trailing edges, curving inwards; pointed tips; distinct notch in centre; often seen.

**Humpback Whale:** The tail fluke has a broad, irregular, knobbly trailing edge; distinct notch; usually black on top and variable white patches underneath; each whale has a different pattern; often seen.

**Bryde's Whale:** The tail fluke is relatively broad; distinct notch in centre; slightly concave trailing edges.

### Bryde's Whale
*Balaenoptera edeni*
(13 - 14 m)

Some of these whales are resident off the southern coast all year, while others migrate to equatorial waters. They are often seen 6 - 15 km offshore, in small groups of 5 - 6. They swim much faster than Southern Right Whales, often darting here and there to chase small fish such as anchovy, pilchard and squid. They also eat plankton.

*The flippers are large, paddle-shaped and often seen.*

*No dorsal fin*

*The flippers are very long, about 1/3 of body length; knobs on leading edge, notches on trailing edge; often seen; usually black on top and white underneath.*

*The flippers are slender and short, about 1/10 of body length; pointed tips; not often seen.*

**Humpback Whale:** The dorsal fin is a low, stubby fin with hump in front, very variable; small humps behind fin towards tail.

**Bryde's Whale:** The dorsal fin is prominent, erect and hooked; shark-like; variable; trailing edge sometimes frayed; situated about 2/3 of the way back along the body.

# Sea Mammals

## Whales and Dolphins

Whales and dolphins are called Cetaceans, 37 species of which occur off southern Africa. Cetaceans surface to breathe air, blowing out a spout of air and water vapour as they do so. They can see both above and below the surface of the water by changing the lens shape in their eyes. There are two groups of Cetaceans, those with teeth, which mainly eat fish and squid, and those with comb-like baleen plates to strain plankton from the water. Both whales and dolphins jump out of the water (breach), and some whales slap the water with their tail flukes and flippers.

◄ **Orca**
*Orcinus orca* (M 8,8 m; F 7,9 m)
Orca whales are often seen floating belly-up or jumping clear out of the water. They hu in packs catching fish, squid, birds, seals and dolphins, and are sometimes called 'Killer Whales'. They wi even attack large whale but are not known to attack people. Like some other Cetaceans, they ta care of injured companions.

**Minke Whale** ▲
*Balaenoptera acutorostrata* (9,2 - 9,8 m)
Minke Whales migrate to the Antarctic where they aggregate in large numbers during summer to feed on krill. Some females and calves may stay in warmer waters, where small fish become part of their diet. They are the smallest and most abundant of the baleen whales and are usually spotted when they leap clear out of the water, ending their breech in a huge splash. Promontories along the coast are usually the best places to spot this whale. Minke whales may form a large part of the Killer Whale's diet in the Antarctic.

▼ **False Killer Whale**
*Pseudorca crassidens* (5,5 m)
Smaller and darker than true killer whales, these blunt-nosed whales may be seen jumping out of th water in a flat, low arc. They eat mainly fish and squid and live in small groups. They are attracted to boats, but d not usually follow them as they are slow swimmers.

◄ **Cape Fur Seal**
*Arctocephalus pusillus pusillus* (M 2,2 m; F 1,6 m)
Fur Seals have thick coats of dark-brown to golden. These superb swimmers eat mainly fish, but also squid and mud prawns. Seals can also move on land and are quite skilled climbers. When hauling themselves out of the sea, they use the waves to help them up onto rocks.

### ◄Common Dolphin
*Delphinus delphis* (2,5 m)
These streamlined dolphins have a figure-of-eight pattern on each side, which is sometimes tinged with yellow. There is also a thin black line from the corner of the mouth to the flipper. They live in 'pods' of 20 to several hundred animals, following well-defined routes along the coast. They usually feed in deeper waters on fish, squid and cuttlefish, and can swim up to 20 knots, often following ships for long distances.

### Humpback Dolphin
*Sousa plumbea* (2,8 m)
Recognised by the hump below their back fin, they are hardy and less playful than other dolphins. They seldom jump, surf or follow ships. They form small groups, usually of 3 - 7, and catch fish around rocky reefs.

### ▼ Bottlenosed Dolphin ▲
*Tursiops truncatus* (2,6 - 3,3 m)
Bottlenosed Dolphins have a thin, pale line running from the eye to the flipper and short, stout snouts. They are usually seen off the coast surfing in the waves or feeding on fish and squid. They live in organised social groups of 10 - 60. They hunt together, herding the fish into a small area to catch them more easily.

### Echolocation

*Common Dolphin*

Dolphins and other toothed whales navigate and find their food using echolocation. This means they produce high-frequency, pulsed sounds (clicks) which bounce back off solid objects, so they can find out where they are. They communicate with each other using a variety of other sounds – groans, moans and whistles. Baleen whales, such as the humpbacks, produce very low frequency sounds ('songs') that travel more than 10 km. These sounds are produced, not by a vocal cord, but via the respiratory system, especially the nasal cavity. The underwater sonar used by many ships and submarines can interfere with the echolocation and communication channels of Cetaceans, making it difficult for them to find their mates and locate feeding grounds.

*Ecolocation - the above illustrates how, by use of high-frequency sounds, this Common Dolphin locates its food in the form of Zebra fish (page 70).*

# MAINLY MARINE FISH

The greatest mass of marine fish is found in the surface waters of the open sea. The greatest diversity is found in the coastal zone, where the fish display an amazing variety of form and colour. Marine fish are divided into two main groups, bony and cartilaginous fishes – the difference being in the structure of the skeleton.

## CARTILAGINOUS FISH

Cartilaginous fish include the sharks, rays, sandsharks and sawfishes. Their skeletons consist of cartilage, which is what separates them from the bony fish (pages 68 - 71). They are all carnivorous with exceptionally good senses of hearing and smell (some sharks can hear up to a kilometre away). They also have a remarkable electrical detection system, which is very sensitive to vibrations and assists hunting.

*People have used the oceans' renewable fish resources from the earliest times. The pressure on marine resources has increased so greatly in recent times that many fish species have suffered from over-fishing. The marine ecosystem is fragile, and its use as a sustainable resource must be based on an understanding of the biological processes that govern life in the oceans.*

**Comparison of sizes**

*Human*

*Common Dolphin*

*Great White Shark*

*Southern Right Whale (the same length as 4 elephants head-to-tail)*

**▲ Pyjama Shark (Striped Catsharks)**
*Poroderma africanum*
(95 cm)
These sharks occur only in South Africa. They are usually found in rocky areas with shallow water where they feed at night on small reef fish and octopus.

**Bullray ▼**
*Pteromylaeus bovinus*
(disc width 1,8 m)
Bullrays are found in coastal waters and estuaries. They can be seen on the surface, sometimes leaping from the water. They feed on crabs and mussels, grinding the shells with their flat teeth.

**◄ Sandshark (Lesser Guitarfish)**
*Rhinobatos annulatus*
(1,2 m)
Sandsharks are found in the surf-zone and near estuaries. They often lie hidden, burrowing below the sand. They feed on crabs, sea-lice and small fish which they crush with their tiny teeth.

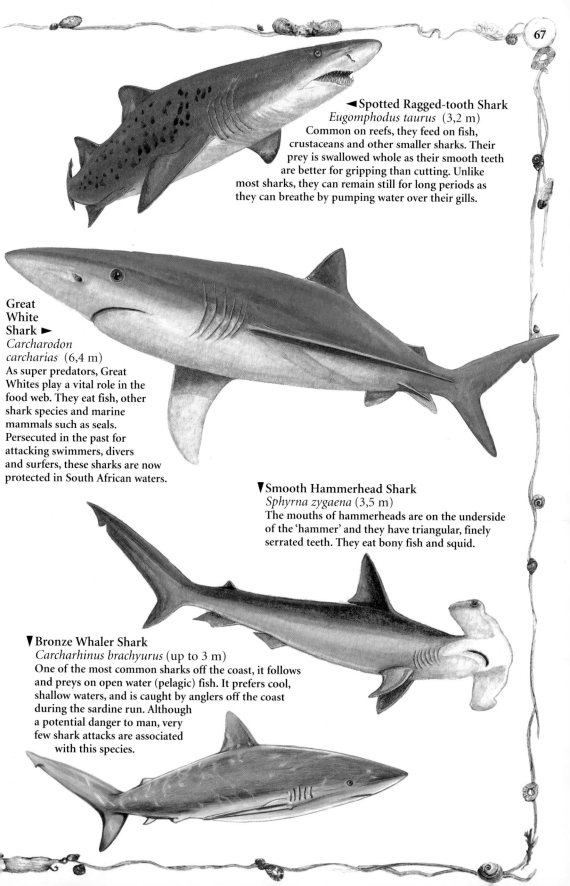

◄ Spotted Ragged-tooth Shark
*Eugomphodus taurus* (3,2 m)
Common on reefs, they feed on fish,
crustaceans and other smaller sharks. Their
prey is swallowed whole as their smooth teeth
are better for gripping than cutting. Unlike
most sharks, they can remain still for long periods as
they can breathe by pumping water over their gills.

Great
White
Shark ►
*Carcharodon
carcharias* (6,4 m)
As super predators, Great
Whites play a vital role in the
food web. They eat fish, other
shark species and marine
mammals such as seals.
Persecuted in the past for
attacking swimmers, divers
and surfers, these sharks are now
protected in South African waters.

▼ Smooth Hammerhead Shark
*Sphyrna zygaena* (3,5 m)
The mouths of hammerheads are on the underside
of the 'hammer' and they have triangular, finely
serrated teeth. They eat bony fish and squid.

▼ Bronze Whaler Shark
*Carcharhinus brachyurus* (up to 3 m)
One of the most common sharks off the coast, it follows
and preys on open water (pelagic) fish. It prefers cool,
shallow waters, and is caught by anglers off the coast
during the sardine run. Although
a potential danger to man, very
few shark attacks are associated
with this species.

# MAINLY MARINE FISH

## SHOALING BONY FISH

Bony fish have this name because their skeletons are made up of bone. But they also differ from the cartilaginous fish (see page 66) in having a swim bladder. This allows the fish to maintain neutral buoyancy at different depths without expending too much energy. The fish illustrated on these pages are those occurring in large shoals in open waters. Shoaling behaviour is a defence against predators which makes an attack on any individual difficult. It also means the predator must spend longer searching for its prey. Many of these fish are coloured dark on the top and pale on the bottom, which provides camouflage to escape predation from above and below.

**▼ Cape Anchovy ▲**
*Engraulis japonicus*
(13 cm)
Cape Anchovies are found from the surface of the sea to a depth of 400 m. Being filter-feeders, they sieve planktonic animals from the water. They are an important source of food for marine animals such as dolphins, sharks and seals.

**Chokka (Squid) ►**
*Loligo vulgaris*
(20 - 30 cm)
This abundant and significant predator is also an important food source for fish, sharks, sea birds and people who enjoy it as calamari.

**◄ Elf (Shad)**
*Pomatomus
saltatrix*
(1 m)
Elf are fierce predators with razor-sharp teeth. They feed in shoals on sandy seabeds and reefs eating anchovies, pilchards and pinkies.

**Leervis (Garrick) ►**
*Lichia amia* (1,5 m)
These aggressive, swift fish live as predators, forming small hunting shoals in the wave-zone off beaches and rocky points. Elf is their favourite food.

◄Geelbek▲
*Atractoscion aequidens*
(1,2 m)
Geelbek are common shoaling
fish found in depths of up to 100 m,
close to the bottom of the seabed near
steep ledges or shipwrecks. They eat
maasbanker, mackerel, pilchard and
sometimes squid.

◄Pilchard
*Sardinops sagax*
(30 cm)
These offshore fish
form large shoals and
feed on plankton.
Each year sea currents
and gamefish, such as Tuna,
drive them into the surf-zone, causing
the famous 'sardine run'.

◄▼Southern
Mullet (Harder)
*Liza richardsonii*
(40 cm)
These fish can be seen off rocky
points and sandy beaches. They feed
on phytoplankton and dead plant
and animal matter.

▲Cape Yellowtail►
*Seriola lalandi*
(1 - 1,5 m)
Common gamefish living mainly
in the Atlantic, they migrate up the
east coast each winter, following the
'sardine run'. They form large offshore
shoals up to depths of 50 m.

Strepie►
*Sarpa salpa*
(30 cm)
Strepies live inshore,
preferring cooler water.
Feeding shoals move in and
out of shallow water with the tides.
The young feed on planktonic animals
and, when larger, on red seaweeds.

# MAINLY MARINE FISH

## OTHER BONY FISH

The bony fish illustrated on these pages are those found in deep water, like the Kingklip, but mostly those that live along the rocky reefs and may be seen when snorkelling or scuba diving. The rocky reefs provide shelter, food and nesting sites for the fish. Caves or seaweed growing on the rocks provide ideal hiding places to escape predation, or places of ambush.

◀ **Blacktail (Dassie)**
*Diplodus sargus capensis* (40 cm)
Blacktail like turbulent water and rocky shores, and move in and out with the tides in small shoals. Their food includes seaweed, mussels, sponges and red-bait.

◀ **Zebra**
*Diplodus cervinus hottentotus* (50 cm)
These fish are found in rocky areas to a depth of 60 m. Adult fish feed on seaweed, small crabs and tube worms.

◀ **Yellowbelly Rockcod**
*Epinephelus guaza* (1,5 m)
Found near rocky shores and reefs to a depth of 200 m, they feed on small fish and crustaceans, especially crayfish, which they swallow whole.

▼ **Spotted Grunter**
*Pomadasys commersonni* (80 cm)
Living in shallow coastal waters and estuaries, Spotted Grunter feed on worms and shellfish. They blow them out of their burrows with a jet of water forced through their mouths.

▼ **Galjoen**
*Coracinus capensis* (80 cm)
Galjoen are found only in southern Africa and are South Africa's national fish. They are found off rocky shores, and feed on red-bait, seaweed, small mussels and barnacles. They are a protected species.

◄ **Twotone Fingerfin**
*Chirodactylus brachydactylus*
(40 cm)
These fish are found only in the shallow reefs of southern Africa. They feed on mouthfuls of sand, sifting out small crustaceans and molluscs, before discarding the sand through their gill openings.

◄ **Doublesash Butterflyfish**
*Chaetodon marleyi*
(10 - 20 cm)
Usually found in pairs, the adult fish prefer rocky or coral reefs which range in depth from 1 - 120 m. They eat a variety of food including small invertebrates and seaweed.

▲ **Red Roman** ►
*Chrysoblephus laticeps*
(30 - 50 cm)
Red Romans are offshore reef fish found in depths of up to 100 m. They feed on crustaceans, worms, sea urchins and other invertebrates.

**Evileyed Puffer (Blaasop)** ▼
*Amblyrhynchotes honckenii* (30 cm)
These spiny fish often lie buried in sand with only their eyes protruding, ready to ambush prey such as small crabs and slow-swimming fish. Their flesh is poisonous to eat.

**Kingklip** ▼
*Genypterus capensis* (1,5 m)
Kingklip live on the bottom of the sea around offshore banks between depths of 50 - 500 m. They feed on fish and invertebrates, and are one of South Africa's most eaten fish.

**Musselcracker** ►
*Sparodon durbanensis* (1,2 m)
Musselcrackers are large fish found along rocky shores and shallow reefs. They like to feed on mussels which they crush with their powerful jaws and teeth.

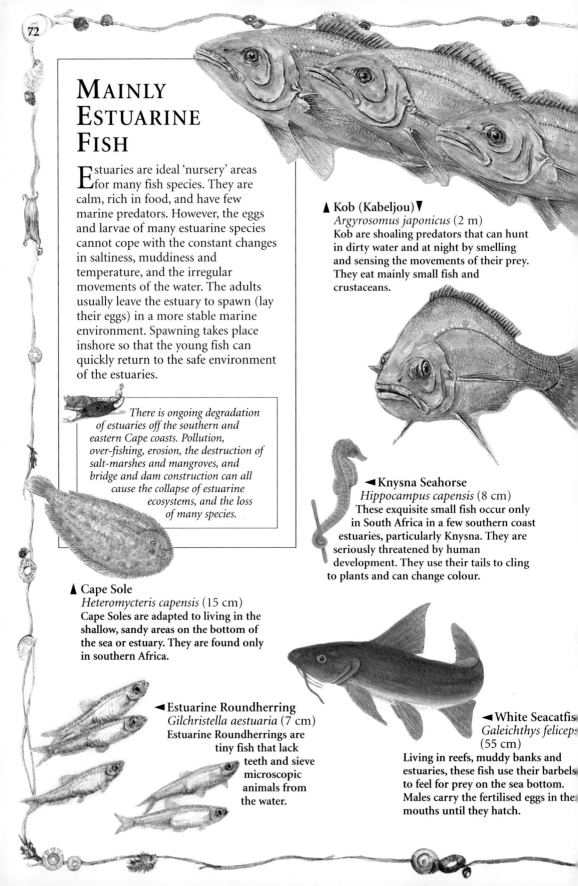

# MAINLY ESTUARINE FISH

Estuaries are ideal 'nursery' areas for many fish species. They are calm, rich in food, and have few marine predators. However, the eggs and larvae of many estuarine species cannot cope with the constant changes in saltiness, muddiness and temperature, and the irregular movements of the water. The adults usually leave the estuary to spawn (lay their eggs) in a more stable marine environment. Spawning takes place inshore so that the young fish can quickly return to the safe environment of the estuaries.

*There is ongoing degradation of estuaries off the southern and eastern Cape coasts. Pollution, over-fishing, erosion, the destruction of salt-marshes and mangroves, and bridge and dam construction can all cause the collapse of estuarine ecosystems, and the loss of many species.*

▲ **Kob (Kabeljou)**▼
*Argyrosomus japonicus* (2 m)
Kob are shoaling predators that can hunt in dirty water and at night by smelling and sensing the movements of their prey. They eat mainly small fish and crustaceans.

◄**Knysna Seahorse**
*Hippocampus capensis* (8 cm)
These exquisite small fish occur only in South Africa in a few southern coast estuaries, particularly Knysna. They are seriously threatened by human development. They use their tails to cling to plants and can change colour.

▲ **Cape Sole**
*Heteromycteris capensis* (15 cm)
Cape Soles are adapted to living in the shallow, sandy areas on the bottom of the sea or estuary. They are found only in southern Africa.

◄**Estuarine Roundherring**
*Gilchristella aestuaria* (7 cm)
Estuarine Roundherrings are tiny fish that lack teeth and sieve microscopic animals from the water.

◄**White Seacatfish**
*Galeichthys feliceps*
(55 cm)
Living in reefs, muddy banks and estuaries, these fish use their barbels to feel for prey on the sea bottom. Males carry the fertilised eggs in their mouths until they hatch.

**Flathead Mullet** ►
*Mugil cephalus*
(80 cm)
Flathead Mullet fish are
often seen jumping out of
the water. They form
large shoals and feed
on dead plant
material.

**White Steenbras** ▼
*Lithognathus lithognathus* (1 m)
Common in shallow water, these fish eat
prawns, shrimps, bloodworms, small
crabs, periwinkles and molluscs. They
blow the prey from their burrows.

◄**Cape
Stumpnose**
*Rhabdosargus
holubi*
(40 cm)
Stumpnose
are common in
shallow coastal water,
and eat plants, molluscs, shrimps and crabs.
They are an important source of food for subsistence
fishermen who live near the estuaries.

*Blowing a
prawn hole*

◄**Longfin Eel**
*Anguilla
mossambica* (1,2 m)
Longfin Eels eat small
invertebrates, crabs, frogs and
fish. After living in freshwater
for 10 years or more, they
return to the Indian
Ocean to breed.

▼ **Cape Silverside**
*Atherina breviceps* (11 cm)
Cape Silverside form shoals and feed on
planktonic animals. They breed in
estuaries and can complete their
whole life cycle in
these systems.

▼ **Knysna Sand Goby**
*Psammogobius knysnaensis* (7 cm)
These fish are usually found on sandy banks,
occurring only in southern Africa.
They breed in estuaries and feed
on small invertebrates.

# INVERTEBRATES

The invertebrates are a huge, diverse group of animals that lack a supporting spinal column. The ones included here are those found inhabiting the sandy beaches and rocky shores. Unlike the rocky shore inhabitants, the animals using the beaches live beneath the sand and are harder to find.

## ROCKY POOLS

Unlike sandy beaches, rocky shores offer shelter and solid foundations on which animals and plants can anchor themselves. Different groups of animals live in different zones up the rocky shore, according to how long they can survive out of the water.

For example, limpets prefer the lower shores, barnacles and mussels prefer the mid-shore, and periwinkles, which can survive out of the water for long periods, are found at the top, near the high-tide mark.

The ideal time to study the rocks and pools is when they are exposed at low tide. An overcast day is the perfect opportunity to spend a few hours on the rocks discovering new life at the coast.

▼ Red Starfish
*Patiria granifera* (width 80 mm)
Deep-orange to red in colour, the surface of these starfish resembles overlapping tiles. They feed on dead plant and animal matter.

▼ Spiny Starfish
*Marthasterias glacialis* (width 20 cm)
Spiny Starfish are greedy predators that hunch over mussels prising apart the shells with their feet. The starfish then push out their stomachs to digest them. They also feed on red-bait.

◄ Cushion Star
*Patiriella exigua* (width 20 mm)
Coloured to blend into the rocks, these starfish feed by pushing their stomachs onto the rocks through their centred, underside mouths, where they digest microscopic algae.

White Mussel ▼
*Donax serra* (88 mm)
Common on sandy beaches, White Mussels burrow just below the surface of the sand. One siphon sucks in water for filter-feeding, while the other expels waste water.

Angular Surf Clam ▼
*Scissodesma spengleri* (11,3 cm)
Surf Clams burrow just below the surface of the sand. They are filter-feeders, sucking in water and filtering out food particles as they pass over their gills.

◄ Eye Limpet
*Patella oculus* (10 cm)
Eye Limpets eat algae. Larger ones attack small predators, such as whelks or starfish, by slamming their shells down on them (page 79).

◄ African Periwinkle
*Nodilittorina africana knysnaensis* (10 mm)
Living near the high-water mark, African Periwinkles avoid drying out by closing their shells with a horny trapdoor, or by hanging from rocks on sticky mucus threads (page 79).

Pear Limpet ▼
*Patella cochlear* (70 mm)
Pear Limpets withstand buffeting waves by clinging tightly to the rocks. They scrape the algae off the rocks with long rasping tongues (page 79).

◄ **Red-bait**
*Pyura stolonifera*
(height 15 cm)
These sea-squirts live in
crowded groups at
the low-tide
zone,
enjoying the
wave action.
They are the
only animals
to make
cellulose in large
quantities.

**Common Octopus ▼**
*Octopus vulgaris* (60 cm)
Octopuses are molluscs that are related
to snails. They can change colour for
protection. They eat crabs, lobsters and
shellfish, and hide in rock cavities.

▼ **Brown Mussel**
*Perna perna* (12,5 cm)
These are edible mussels that
secure themselves to rocks by
tough threads formed by a
gland in the 'foot'. They
are filter-feeders,
sieving food from
the water.

▼ **False Plum Anemone**
*Pseudactinia flagellifera*
(width 50 - 100 mm)
Like other anemones, these animals
cling to rocks with their muscles
and a sticky mucus, while standing
on a fleshy 'foot'. They can move
about slowly, but cannot close up.

◄ **Cape
Urchin**
*Parechinus
angulosus* (width 60 mm)
Colourful Cape Urchins feed on
seaweed and microalgae. They use
empty shells as 'hats' for protection
against the sun (page 78).

**Plum Anemone ▼**
*Actinia equina*
(width 20 mm)
Plum Anemones are
animals that feed on
shrimps and fish which
they catch with the help
of stinging cells in their
tentacles. To survive out of water
they close up, looking like ripe plums.

**Cape Rock Oyster ►**
*Striostrea
margaritacea*
(18 cm)
Oysters live at the
high-tide level,
cemented to the rocks.
They filter-feed, straining
food particles and micro-
organisms from the water.
The Knysna Oyster
Company grows oysters
commercially.

▼ **Three-spot Swimming Crab**
*Ovalipes trimaculatus*
(width 40 mm)
Living beneath the sand in
the surf-zone, they
feed on mussels and
snails. They smash the
shells open with their claws
and then shred the flesh.

# INVERTEBRATES

## SHORELINE, MUD FLATS AND ESTUARIES

Many shoreline sand-dwellers become active at night. Others move up and down the beach with the waves and tides. They depend on food washed up by the waves and blown in by the wind. Their environment is constantly changing.

The mud flats around estuaries are more stable places to live. They support more animals because they are rich in nutrients washed down by the rivers. The animals living here have adapted to coping with changing salt levels in the water.

◄ **Horse Mussel**
*Atrina squamifera* (39 cm)
Horse Mussels are fragile animals that lie buried in the sand or mud with the sharp, slightly open back edges of their shells just visible above the surface.

**Bloodworm** ►
*Arenicola loveni* (80 cm)
Bloodworms feed on dead plant or animal matter and micro-organisms by drawing water into their U-shaped burrows. If damaged, they 'bleed' a red fluid. They are eaten by many fish.

**Cuttlefish** ▲
*Sepia vermiculata*
(body 15 cm)
The 'shell' of this mollusc, a chalky cuttlebone inside the body, keeps it afloat (page 78). Cuttlefish swim by jet propulsion, and catch fish by shooting out their suckered tentacles.

**Pencil-bait** ▼
*Solen capensis* (16 cm)
Burrowing into the sand, these molluscs use long siphons to filter food from the water. When their siphons are drawn in, a key-hole shape is left in the sand.

**Heart Urchin** ►
*Echinocardium cordatum*
(40 mm)
All sea urchins' bodies are protected by a fragile shell with spines. Heart Urchins' mouths have a scoop-like lip for feeding on dead plant and animal matter.

▼ **Pansy Shell Urchin**
*Echinodiscus bisperforatus* (90 mm)
These are the flat, biscuit-like shells of dead sea urchins. When alive, they lie buried in the sand and feed on small organisms and dead plant and animal matter.

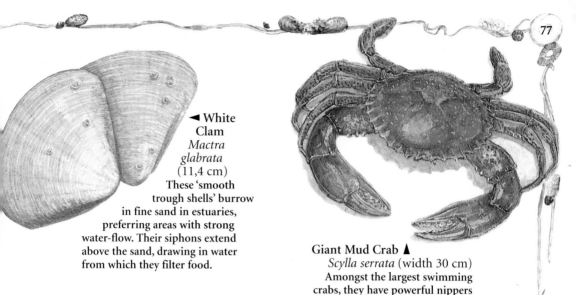

◄ **White Clam**
*Mactra glabrata*
(11,4 cm)
These 'smooth trough shells' burrow in fine sand in estuaries, preferring areas with strong water-flow. Their siphons extend above the sand, drawing in water from which they filter food.

**Giant Mud Crab** ▲
*Scylla serrata* (width 30 cm)
Amongst the largest swimming crabs, they have powerful nippers and paddle-shaped back legs. They come out of the sand or mud at sunset to feed on molluscs and shellfish.

**Common Sand Hermit Crab** ►
*Diogenes brevirostris*
(30 mm)
Living in empty shells, they use their larger left nipper as a door. They are scavengers but can also filter food from the water with feathery 'arms'.

**Crown Crab** ▼
*Hymenosoma orbiculare* (15 mm)
Abundant in estuaries, where they live in sandbanks, these pale crabs are mottled by brown microalgae. They feed on small shellfish.

◄ **Marsh Crab**
*Sesarma catenata*
(25 mm)
They are common crabs that burrow in sand and mud flats near the high-tide mark. They suck in mud and sand particles, to feed on rotting plant and animal matter.

**Estuarine Mudprawn** ▼
*Upogebia africana*
(40 mm)
Living in muddy sand in estuaries, these prawns pump water through their U-shaped burrows, filtering out food particles. Fishermen collect them for bait.

**Sand Prawn** ▲
*Callianassa kraussi* (60 mm)
Found in estuaries where the water current is stronger, Sand Prawns live in deep burrows and feed by sifting the sand for plant and animal matter.

# INVERTEBRATES

## ALONG THE DRIFTLINE

The driftline is the only part of the beach that is reached by waves at high tide. It is a fascinating place to wander and discover the new treasures brought out by the sea. As in all natural systems, plants and animals are continuously dying, while new ones are born to take their place in the life cycle. Crabs and other scavengers may be spotted moving amongst the debris. They feed on the dead matter, thereby recycling nutrients back into the system.

*Top-side*

◄ **Brown Mussel**
*Perna perna* (12,5 cm
The taller, narrower shells are from faster growing mussels, from below the tidal-zone. The smaller, triangular shells are from crowded, intertidal beds of mussels (page 75).

*Under-side*

◄ **Cuttlefish/Cuttlebone**
(30 - 170 mm)
This is the internal chalky plate which once supported a cuttlefish (page 76) and allowed it to control its buoyancy. They are very light and are often washed ashore after the animals die.

▲ **Horn-eyed Ghost C**
*Ocypode ceratophthaln*
(width 40 m
Ghost Crabs dig very deep ho high up on sheltered beaches. T come out at low tide to scavenge dead animals and pla

◄ **Cape Urchin**
*Parechinus angulosus*
(60 mm)
These are the left-over shells of the sea urchin (page 75).

◄ **Common Shore Crab**
**(Rocky Shore Crab)**
*Cyclograpsus punctatus*
(width 30 mm)
Common, but seldom seen, these crabs hide under stones high up the beach. They scavenge at night during low tide, feeding mostly on seaweed, but also on dead animals.

*Top-side*

*Under-side*

◄ **Variegated Topshell** ▼
*Oxystele variegata*
(25 mm)
These winkles use rough file-like 'tongues' to scrape algae off rocks. When young, they live lower down on rocky shores, moving up the beach as they get bigger.

*Under-side*

*Top-side*

**Pink-lipped Topshell** ▲ ►
*Oxystele sinensis* (45 mm)
These winkles feed on algae and live along rocky shores. They look like spinning tops.

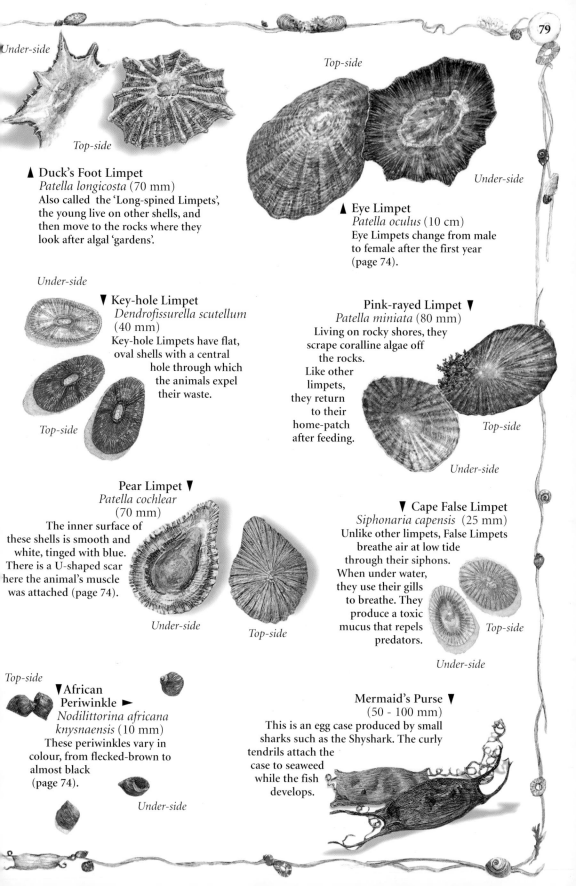

*Under-side*

*Top-side*

▲ **Duck's Foot Limpet**
*Patella longicosta* (70 mm)
Also called the 'Long-spined Limpets',
the young live on other shells, and
then move to the rocks where they
look after algal 'gardens'.

*Top-side*

*Under-side*

▲ **Eye Limpet**
*Patella oculus* (10 cm)
Eye Limpets change from male
to female after the first year
(page 74).

*Under-side*

▼ **Key-hole Limpet**
*Dendrofissurella scutellum*
(40 mm)
Key-hole Limpets have flat,
oval shells with a central
hole through which
the animals expel
their waste.

*Top-side*

**Pink-rayed Limpet** ▼
*Patella miniata* (80 mm)
Living on rocky shores, they
scrape coralline algae off
the rocks.
Like other
limpets,
they return
to their
home-patch
after feeding.

*Top-side*

*Under-side*

**Pear Limpet** ▼
*Patella cochlear*
(70 mm)
The inner surface of
these shells is smooth and
white, tinged with blue.
There is a U-shaped scar
here the animal's muscle
was attached (page 74).

*Under-side*

*Top-side*

▼ **Cape False Limpet**
*Siphonaria capensis* (25 mm)
Unlike other limpets, False Limpets
breathe air at low tide
through their siphons.
When under water,
they use their gills
to breathe. They
produce a toxic
mucus that repels
predators.

*Top-side*

*Under-side*

*Top-side*

▼**African
Periwinkle** ►
*Nodilittorina africana
knysnaensis* (10 mm)
These periwinkles vary in
colour, from flecked-brown to
almost black
(page 74).

*Under-side*

**Mermaid's Purse** ▼
(50 - 100 mm)
This is an egg case produced by small
sharks such as the Shyshark. The curly
tendrils attach the
case to seaweed
while the fish
develops.

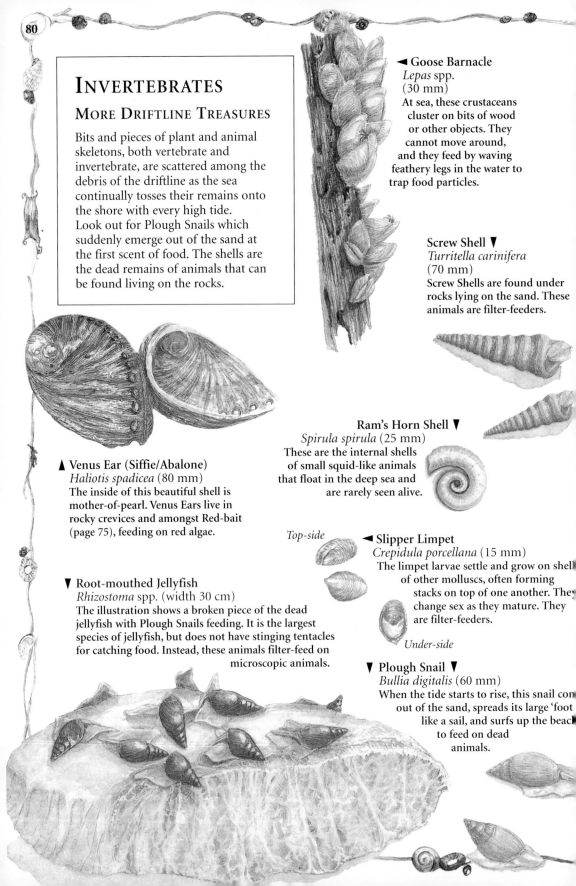

# INVERTEBRATES

## MORE DRIFTLINE TREASURES

Bits and pieces of plant and animal skeletons, both vertebrate and invertebrate, are scattered among the debris of the driftline as the sea continually tosses their remains onto the shore with every high tide. Look out for Plough Snails which suddenly emerge out of the sand at the first scent of food. The shells are the dead remains of animals that can be found living on the rocks.

◄ **Goose Barnacle**
*Lepas* spp.
(30 mm)
At sea, these crustaceans cluster on bits of wood or other objects. They cannot move around, and they feed by waving feathery legs in the water to trap food particles.

**Screw Shell** ▼
*Turritella carinifera*
(70 mm)
Screw Shells are found under rocks lying on the sand. These animals are filter-feeders.

▲ **Venus Ear (Siffie/Abalone)**
*Haliotis spadicea* (80 mm)
The inside of this beautiful shell is mother-of-pearl. Venus Ears live in rocky crevices and amongst Red-bait (page 75), feeding on red algae.

**Ram's Horn Shell** ▼
*Spirula spirula* (25 mm)
These are the internal shells of small squid-like animals that float in the deep sea and are rarely seen alive.

*Top-side*

◄ **Slipper Limpet**
*Crepidula porcellana* (15 mm)
The limpet larvae settle and grow on shell of other molluscs, often forming stacks on top of one another. They change sex as they mature. They are filter-feeders.

*Under-side*

▼ **Root-mouthed Jellyfish**
*Rhizostoma* spp. (width 30 cm)
The illustration shows a broken piece of the dead jellyfish with Plough Snails feeding. It is the largest species of jellyfish, but does not have stinging tentacles for catching food. Instead, these animals filter-feed on microscopic animals.

▼ **Plough Snail** ▼
*Bullia digitalis* (60 mm)
When the tide starts to rise, this snail com out of the sand, spreads its large 'foot like a sail, and surfs up the beac to feed on dead animals.

**Smooth Turban Shell** ►
*Turbo cidaris cidaris* (30 mm)
These snails live in rock
pools or under boulders,
along the mid-shore. They
eat plants.

*Operculum
(shell lid)*

◄ **Mottled Necklace
Shell**
*Natica tecta* (41 mm)
The snails feed on mussels.
They secrete acids to drill holes
into the shells of their prey.

◄ **Alikreukel
(Giant Periwinkle)**
*Turbo sarmaticus* (10 cm)
These molluscs can close their shells
using a white 'lid' which prevents water-
loss. They live in rock pools and feed on
algae at night.

**Furry-ridged Triton** ▼
*Cymatium cutaceum africanum*
(50 mm)
The shell shapes are
variable. When alive,
these whelk shells are
coated with a brown
'fur', and are often
found amongst Red-
bait (page 75) on
which they may feed.

**Striped
Burnupena** ►
*Burnupena
pubescens* (50 mm)
These whelks live in the subtidal-
zone. They eat wounded or dead
animals which they find by detecting
the scent carried in water currents.

◄ **Bluebottle**
*Physalia physalia*
(float 50 mm long,
tentacles 10 m or 30 cm
when contracted)
Each Bluebottle is a colony of four
independent specialised animals living
together. They float on the surface of the open sea,
relying on winds and currents to move them
around. Their long tentacles, which are used to
catch prey, shoot out stinging barbs when touched.

**Bubble-raft
Shell** ►
*Janthina janthina*
(34 mm)
Bubble-rafts are the shells
of violet snails that drift
around the open sea, held
up by a float of bubbles.
They feed on bluebottles.

▼ **Beach Hopper (Sand Hopper)**
*Talorchestia capensis* (10 - 12 mm)
Beach Hoppers are crustaceans that feed
on seaweed at night. They are often
found under driftwood and
become very active when
disturbed.

**Tick Shell** ▼
*Nassarius kraussianus* (7 - 10 mm)
These tiny snails live in mud banks and
feed on small bivalves or dead
animal and plant matter. They
sense their food by holding
their siphons erect, like an
elephant's trunk.

*Top-side*

*Under-side*

# PLANTS AND INSECTS

The climate and geology of an area are the main factors determining the vegetation types and plant diversity occurring there. The plain between the coast and the mountain slopes, stretching from George to Tsitsikamma, enjoys high year-round rainfall that allows the growth of huge trees in indigenous forests. Near the coast and on the mountains, conditions are not favourable for closed canopy, large tree-growth. Here, Cape fynbos, which is adapted to the harsher conditions, thrives. Numerous rivers flow from the mountains towards the sea, and provide additional habitats. These habitats harbour microhabitats, which offer a great variety of food shelter and breeding sites for animals.

A number of insects have been illustrated with the plants. They all interact with the plants in some way, and are associated with certain habitat types.

*Sizes given refer to the height of the average adult plant, to the wingspan of butterflies or to the body length of other insects. Where appropriate the month in which these plants flower is given. The national tree number is also given after the size of each species.*

*The King Protea, South Africa's national flower, in all its glorious majesty*

# FORESTS

South Africa's dry climate means that less than 0,5% of the country is covered in indigenous forests. The magnificent forests of the Knysna-Tsitsikamma region are amongst our finest. They are a breathtakingly beautiful, living monument to millions of years of natural history. They show how the Coastal Plain eco-system looked and functioned before urbanisation and industrialisation.

## THE BIGGER TREES

Many of the trees, particularly yellowwoods, ironwood and stinkwood grow to a massive size, even by world standards. Because of this, their timber has been important in shaping the human history of the southern Cape, and relatively few of the huge trees remain today. However a number of impressive yellowwoods can be seen driving along the N2 between Nature's Valley and Storms River, where there is a patch of very valuable indigenous forest.

*It is important to be pro-active in the protection of precious, irreplaceable forest patches. No single reason for human advancement can possibly, long-term, overshadow the need to keep the very little forest we have left.*

◀▼ **Cape Chestnut**
*Calodendrum capensis* Oct - Dec
(7 - 20 m) 256
Evergreen
This tree has smooth, grey bark with white and orange patches, and large, dark, strong-smelling leaves. Its large flowers vary from white to pale-pink. The seeds are in woody, knobbly capsules. It grows along the coastal strip, in river valleys and in forests.

▼ **Broom Cluster Fig** ▶
*Ficus sur* Sep - Mar
(15 - 25 m) 50
Semi-deciduous
This distinctive fig, well-named for its unusual bunches of fruit, naturally occurs in protected ravines near the coast. It was a favoured species for making fire by frictioning two "fire sticks" – one of its earliest names.

◀ **Forest Tree-fern** ▼
*Cyathea capensis*
No flowers (5 m) 2 Evergreen
The trunk is covered with blackish leaf-stubs and scales. The large leaves can be up to 3 metres long. It grows in moist conditions and in high forests. The Common Tree Fern is similar, and is often found on forest edges and along grassy mountain streams.

*Under-side of leaf-frond, showing brown spores*

**Cicada**
Family Cicadidae (45 mm)
With their piercing mouth parts, these insects feed on tree juices (sap). The shrill droning noise often heard from trees and bushes is made by male cicadas. Females lay eggs in slits in tree bark.

◄ ▼ Small-leaved Yellowwood
(Outeniqua Yellowwood)
*Podocarpus falcatus*
Sep - May (20 - 60 m)
16 Evergreen
The *Podocarpus* genus is South
Africa's national tree. It has smooth
bark which flakes off in irregular pieces.
Bats and birds eat its yellow, fleshy fruit.
It grows in ravines and in mountain and
coastal, swamp forests. The timber is
valuable, and in the past, the trunks were
used for ship masts.

◄ Broad-leaved
Yellowwood ▲
(Real Yellowwood)
*Podocarpus latifolius*
Jul - Sep (20 - 30 m)
18 Evergreen
The bark varies from yellow-
brown to dark-brown and peels
off in long strips. The cones are
pink on male trees, and bright red
on female trees. The pale-yellow
timber has always been highly valued,
especially as flooring in old
Cape houses.

◄ Small
Ironwood ►
*Olea capensis*
Aug - Feb (10 - 40 m)
618 Deciduous
The bark darkens with age and, if
damaged, it 'bleeds' a slimy, black
gum. It has very small, white or cream,
scented flowers, and the olive-like
purple fruit is eaten by many birds
and animals. In the past, this hard, grained
wood was used for railway sleepers.

Black Stinkwood ▼ ►
*Ocotea bullata*
Dec - Feb (8 - 30 m)
118 Evergreen
When young, the bark of this
tree is smooth with a
variety of coloured
patches. Older trees
have rougher grey-
brown bark. Its large,
oblong leaves have
'blisters' at their base,
and smell strongly if
crushed. The freshly cut
wood has an unpleasant
smell. However, its beautiful
timber is often used to
make furniture.

◄ Bracket Fungus
(many species commonly known
under the name) (size varies)
This is generally known as Bracket Fungi
because the fruit-body projects like a
bracket from either dead wood, branches
or tree trunks. It plays an integral part in
the decomposition of wood.

# FORESTS

## MORE BIG TREES

From the early 1800s, trees were used for building ships, houses and furniture, and for fuel. It soon became necessary to protect the forests legally. Although much of the wood-supply now comes from commercial plantations, indigenous forests still need protection from human activities, such as building, farming and even recreation. However, hiking, walking, cycling, horse riding, birding, tree spotting, swimming and picnicking in our forests are a wonderful way to spend time in the Garden Route.

▲ **Heart-leaved Grape (Common Forest Grape)** ▼
*Rhoicissus tomentosa* Oct - Dec Deciduous
(3 - 7 m as a small tree; as a climber can reach the top of 20 m high trees) 456.5
The leaves are dark-green above and hairy below. Young vines attach themselves to small trees, and as the trees grow they are lifted up into the forest canopy. Flowers grow in dense heads and are small, creamy-green. Birds eat the purple fruit (Jan - Apr).

◄ **Western Keurboom** ▼
*Virgilia oroboides* Aug - Sep or Dec - Jan (10 m) 221 Deciduous
It has brown-grey, smooth bark and leaves with small leaflets – glossy green above and hairy below. Sprays of pink-mauve flowers change to long, flat, brown, velvety pods. It grows in coastal forest edges and river valleys.

◄ ▼ Cape-beech
*Rapanea melanaphloes*
Jun - Dec
(5 - 20 m) 578
Evergreen
This can be relatively easy to identify because younger stems and branches are pale grey, and covered with small, flat knobs, resembling ostrich skin. It is widespread in mountain ranges and forests in eastern South Africa, and from Cape Town to the Limpopo.

▼ **Cape-ash**
*Ekebergia capensis*
Sep - Nov (10 - 30 m) 298 Evergreen
Although relatively rare, growing naturally as far south as the Garden Route, it is planted extensively in all the main towns as a street and garden tree. Its unusual shaped, asymmetrical compound leaves and bunched, red, berry-fruit make it easily confused with Wild-plum (*Harpephyllum caffrum*).

**White-elder ▶**
*Platylophus*
*tripfoliatus*
(25 m) 141
Evergreen

Three of these four trees (**White-elder,**
**White-ironwood** and **Red Currant-rhus**)
have **three-leaflet compound leaves.**
The **Red-elder** has 3 - 5 pairs of leaflets and
an end leaflet. They are all beautiful trees, worth
finding, and are fairly common along the
Garden Route. The Red Currant-rhus is likely to
be found at forest margins as a pioneer plant, or
in gardens, in both instances growing from bird
droppings. White-ironwood is in similar forest
habitat, and the strong lemon smell from
crushed leaves is diagnostic. Both White-elder
and Red-elder need high levels of moisture,
and particularly the Red-elder is found
leaning over streams and rivers. The
White-elder is endemic, and makes a
wonderful honey that is worth
searching for at local farm stalls.

**▲ Red-elder ▼**
*Cunonia*
*capensis*
Mar - May
(up to 30 m) 140
Evergreen

**▼ Red Currant-rhus ▼**
*Rhus chirindensis*
Nov - Dec (6 - 10 m)
380 Evergreen

**White-ironwood ▲**
*Vepris lanceolata*
Dec - Mar
(15 m) 261
Evergreen

**◀ Forest Nuxia ▼**
**(Forest Elder)**
*Nuxia floribunda*
May - Aug
(3 - 10 m) 634 Evergreen
The bark of this small tree is
pale-grey, smooth and
powdery. It bears sprays of
tiny, fragrant, cream-white
flowers, and has small egg-shaped, creamy-brown
fruit which, when mature, split into four, releasing
the fine seed (Jun - Oct). It grows in evergreen
forests and forest edges. The
pale-yellow wood is hard
and heavy, and it was used
to make wagons.

**Assegai ▼**
*Curtisia dentata*
Oct - Mar (15 m) 570 Evergreen
The first reference to this tree in the Cape is
in a forest survey of 1662. There the
name used is the same as that used
for spears, by Jan van Riebeeck in
1652, *"hassegaayen"*. From the
earliest days timber was prized by
colonists for building and
wagon-making, as well as the
leaves for tanning. It is no
wonder that many of the older,
larger trees were destroyed. To
find this tree, keep a look out for
the spectacularly rigid, glossy,
spikily serrated leaves
on lower-level shoots.

# FORESTS

## BUSHES AND FLOWERING PLANTS

In many of the more open patches, where old trees have fallen, sunlight sprinkles across the lower layers, and allows bushes and flowering plants to thrive. Here birding is more likely to be successful too.

◄ **Tree-fuschia** ▼
*Halleria lucida*
May - Dec
(2 - 3 m) 670 Evergreen
A shrub or small tree, occasionally much larger, the Tree-fuschia occurs in coastal scrub, forest and rocky mountain slopes. The nectar and fruit are extremely attractive to a wide variety of birds such as sunbirds and bulbuls.

◄ **Wild Pomegranite** ▼
*Burchellia bubalina*
Sep - Dec (2 - 3 m)
688 Evergreen
The unusual shape of the flowers and fruit make this small tree a tree-spotters favourite, and both flowers and fruit attract birds, and therefore birders! Both the botanical name *bubalina* (from the latin *bubalus* - buffalo) and an original Afrikaans name, Buffelshoring, describe the twisted calyx horns on the fruit.

**Poison Star-apple** ▲
*Diospyros dicrophyllua*
Nov - Mar (2 - 3 m)
603 Evergreen
This large bush or small tree is in the same far as the very large, well-loved Lowveld tree, Jack berry (*Diospyros mespiliformis*). Their leaves and fruit are similar. Again the Afrikaans nam 'Tolbos' is interesting, referring to the way fru can spin on the ground, like a top, if it is kicke It is the fruit that is poisonous.

◄ **Winged Candlewood** ▼
(Cherrywood)
*Pterocelastrus tricuspidatus*
Jul - Nov (7 - 25 m)
409 Evergreen
Often seen growing as a shrub, this tree has smooth, dark-brown bark, and thick, leathery, shiny leaves. The young branches, leaves and leaf-stalks are pink to red. Its fragrant flowers are creamy-white and its lobed, 'winged' fruit is bright-yellow. It is often found in dune-scrub, as well as in dry to medium-moist forests.

◄ **Black Witch-hazel** ►
*Trichocladus crinitus* Apr - Aug
(3 - 4 m) 142 Evergreen
This shrub or small tree has smooth bark, and brown hairs on the stems and under-surface of th leaves. It has spider-like heads of cream-green, yellow or orange flowe The fruit forms clusters of hairy, brown-red capsules. It is common in medium-moist for and its wood is white and very hard.

◄ **Hen and Chickens**
*Chlorophytum comosum*
Feb (60 cm)
With long, narrow, wavy leaves,
this plant has branched flower-
stems bearing many white, star-
like flowers. New plants
form at the tips of these
stems, and root quickly
forming large clumps of
connected plants.
It grows in coastal
forests and along
mountain streams.

◄ **Bracken** ►
*Pteridium
aquilinum*
(1 - 3 m) Deciduous
This is a terrestrial fern,
growing in full sunlight
in moist areas on forest
margins and in forest
gaps. It is common in
disturbed habitats, often
forming dense clumps.

*Dried
leaf*

◄ **Spur Flower**
*Plectranthus ecklonii*
Mar - May (1,2 - 2 m)
The Spur Flower is a large straggling
shrub with strong-smelling leaves and
stems. The flowers form a series of
pale and dark purple circular
sprays. It prefers moist places
and deep shade.

◄ **Mosquito**
Family Culicidae
(4 - 10 mm)
Mosquitoes are most active at night,
and feed on nectar and the juice of
ripe fruits. Females have piercing
mouth-parts, and also feed on blood.
Males can be identified by their
feathery antennae. Garden Route
mosquitoes do not transmit malaria.

**Twin Sisters (Cape Primrose)** ►
*Streptocarpus rexii*
Nov - Aug (12 - 24 cm)
The thick, wrinkled, velvety leaves of this plant
lie flat on the ground. It has mauve to dark-
purple flowers, and its seed-pods split in a
spiral. It is found along shady forest streams.

◄ **Blue Lily
(Agapanthus)**
*Agapanthus praecox*
Dec - Apr
(40 - 60 cm)
This species has
long, narrow, dark-
green leaves and blue
to purple, trumpet-
shaped flowers that
grow in a round ball at
the end of the long stem.
It is often found
growing in clumps
on sea cliffs and
in coastal forests.

**Arum Lily** ▼
*Zantedeschia aethiopica*
Mainly Sep - Dec
(1,5 m)
Arum Lilies have fleshy
stalks and glossy, pointed
leaves. The flowers are
usually creamy-white,
with a single
folded petal
around a
bright
yellow rod.
They grow
well in
damp
ground,
often in
large
clusters.

# FYNBOS

Fynbos grows in the Cape Floral Kingdom, the smallest of the world's six floral kingdoms, but with the greatest diversity of plant species. Fire plays an important role in driving the system and maintaining this great diversity.

## INDICATOR SPECIES

The Ericas, Restios and Proteas illustrated on this page are all indicator species of Cape fynbos. Fynbos grows on nutrient-poor, acidic soils. It is characterised by its short scrubby appearance (average 1 - 2 metres). The word fynbos comes from the Dutch description of the small, fine-leaved plants that are common.

*A major threat to fynbos is the spread of alien plants such as Hakea, Black Wattle and pine trees. Other threats include too many fires, often in the wrong season, the planting of large areas of trees for commercial use, and the development of housing estates and farms. The conservation of fynbos is a national priority.*

◄ **Ker Ker (Raasheide)**
*Erica imbricata* July - Dec (30 - 50 cm)
This upright shrublet grows on sandy flats, hills and mountain slopes, and is more abundant west of Mossel Bay. The flowers are usually white, sometimes a dull-pink or red. The dark stamens protrude from inside the petals, giving this Erica a very distinctive, attractive appearance.

**Hairy Erica ►**
*Erica hispidula* Oct - Dec (50 - 80 cm)
This small shrub is very abundant on hills and mountains slopes, and common in sandy, dry places but will grow in damp areas. It is wind- not animal-pollinated. Not needing to attract birds or insects, the flowers are small and inconspicuous. Clouds of pollen may be lifted when walking through stands in full bloom.

◄ **Common Heath**
*Erica sparsa* Dec - Apr (up to 2 m)
Common Heath has small, bell-shaped, pale-pink flowers. It grows on southern slopes of coastal mountains.

◄ **Vlakte Heath**
*Erica coccinea*
Apr - Dec
(0,6 - 1 m)
Vlakte Heath is very common on the southern slopes of the Outeniqua and Tsitsikamma mountains. The flowers are densely packed, coloured green, yellow or red. It is found in moist, sandy places on hills and mountains. The small leaves are grouped in tufts up the branches.

**Erica ►**
*Erica versicolor*
Apr - Jun (1 m)
The small flowers on this tall bush vary in colour according to where they grow. One form has flowers which are tube-shaped, red at the base with green-white tips. Sunbirds visit the bush to eat the nectar from the flowers. It grows on lower mountain slopes.

**King Protea ►**
**(Giant Protea)**
*Protea cynaroides*
All year round
(0,3 - 2 m)
This is South Africa's
national flower. The large
flowers (up to 30 cm across)
vary from cone-shaped to
bowl-shaped, and are various shades
of pink. After a fire the plant
quickly re-grows from its thick,
underground stems.

*(F)*

**◄ Cape Scarab**
**Beetle ►**
*Trichostetha*
*fasicularis* (10 - 20 mm)
These brightly
coloured beetles are
strong flyers.
Adults are often
found looking
for nectar in
Protea flowers,
while the larvae
feed on decaying
vegetable matter.

**Restios**
Family Restionaceae
With over 300 species, Restios are common
in, as well as indicators of, fynbos. Similar
in appearance to grasses, these
reed-like plants in fact belong to
a different plant family. Restios
actually take the place of true
grasses in fynbos vegetation,
and have an important function
as ground cover. Interestingly,
Restios are unisexual, the male
and female being on different
plants. Like all fynbos
vegetation, they are able to
survive fires in many different
ways. They are widely used for
thatching.

**Sugarbush ►**
**(Suikerbossie)**
*Protea repens*
All year round (4,5 m)
The leaves of this Protea are
leathery, and the flowers
vary from white to dark-
pink and have sticky
'scales'. The seeds are
like upside-down ice-
cream cones. It flowers
mainly May - Oct in the west,
Sep - Mar in the eastern regions.
The flowers produce a lot of nectar
which, in the 19th Century, was collected
and boiled to make cough medicine.

*1)*

**◄ Elegant Restio**
*Elegia racemosa*
Dec - Mar (up to 6 cm)

**Thatching Reed ►**
*Thamnochortus*
*erectus*

*(M)*

**▼Pincushion**
*Leucospermum*
*cuneiforme*
Sep - Nov
(1,5 m)
This Protea has
toothed leaves at the
top, and 'warts' at the
base of its stems. The
flowers can be yellow, red
or orange, depending on
the area in which they grow.

**◄ Geelbos ►**
**(Sunshine Cone Bush)**
*Leucadendron salignum*
Jul - Sep (1 - 2 m)
The young leaves are lemon-yellow,
becoming darker green with red
margins and tips. These plants often
cover large areas of mountain slopes
and flats. The flowers are on woody
cones, with the female and male
flowers on separate plants. The winged
seeds stay in woody cones on the plant
until after a fire.

*(F)*

**Pugnaceous Ants ►**
*Anoplolepis custodiens*
These ants bury fynbos
seeds so that the seeds
are able to germinate
successfully after fire.

# FYNBOS

## OTHER FLOWERING PLANTS

An important but often inconspicuous component of fynbos are plants with bulbs. The bulbs, hidden under the soil, go unnoticed until they receive a particular environmental cue, such as rain or fire. The flowers that emerge are often the most beautiful and spectacular found in the fynbos. The bulbs of orchid species are much sought-after by collectors, and have become rare as a result.

**Dune Daisy ►**
*Felicia echinata*
Flowers most of the year (60 cm)
The Dune Daisy is a small shrub seen along the roads and on dunes.

**▼ Citrus Swallowtail ►**
**(Christmas Butterfly)**
*Papilio demodocus*
Visible all year (7 - 9 cm)
These insects are most common during the summer, particularly in December. The caterpillars feed on the leaves of various plants.

*Caterpillar stage*

**◄ Spider Orchid**
*Bartholina ethelae*
Oct - Jan (8 - 15 m)
The small, circular leaf of this plant grows flat on the ground, and it has one stem with a purple flower. It is a rare plant and grows in damp, shady places.

**▼ Green Wood-orchid ►**
*Bonatea speciosa*
Oct - Nov (90 cm)
Wavy-edged, pointed leaves enclose the stem of this orchid which grows in the semi-shade of coastal bush and forest edges. It is pollinated by the Hawk Moth which is attracted to its fragrant green and white flowers.

**Convolvulus Hawk Moth ▲**
*Agrius convolvuli*
Visible at night (8 cm)
These large moths are often seen hovering over flowers, feeding on nectar. When not feeding, they coil their long tongues beneath their heads.

**Praying Mantis ►**
*Sphodiomantis gastica* (20 - 85 mm)
Varying greatly in shape and colour, these insects can look like leaves, grass, flowers or tree bark. They catch insects with their front legs which are held in a 'praying' position.

◀ Duine-
aandblom ▼
*Freesia alba*
Aug - Nov (15 - 30 cm)
This thin-leaved plant has
very fragrant, cream-
yellow flowers tinged
with purple. It grows
in dune-scrub and
even in pure sand
at the edge of
freshwater
lakes.

◀ Golden Orchid
*Disa cornuta*
Sep - Feb (30 - 50 cm)
Found from Humansdorp to
Mossel Bay, the Golden Orchid
grows in full sunlight, on
mountains and sandy places.
The outer hood is a dull purple
but it sparkles golden in the
sunlight. It is densely leafy,
with reddish-purple spots at
the base of the leaves.

Blue Disa ▶
*Disa graminifolia*
Mar - Apr (30 - 60 cm)
When hiking in the Outeniqua
Mountains, look out for the
striking, bright blue flowers.
The Blue Disa is widespread
but not very common.
It prefers higher
mountain slopes,
usually on
rocky soils.

◀ Cluster Disa
*Disa ferruginea*
Feb - Apr (20 - 50 cm)
The Cluster Disa is found
especially in the Montagu and
Robinson Pass areas. Although
it does not produce its own
nectar, it mimics other flower
species that do, and is pollinated
by a specialised butterfly. This
grass-like orchid grows on rocks
in the cloud belt of the
Cape mountains. The bright
red-orange flowers appear before leaves.
It is a protected flower.

Suurkanol ▶
*Chasmanthe aethiopica*
May - Jun (60 cm)
Many scarlet flowers grow on one side of the
flowering stem. Its leaves grow in downward
rows around the stem, and its seeds are
bright orange. In shady embankments it can
form large colonies, growing from the
previous year's 'bulb' and long,
underground shoots.

Watsonia ▼
*Watsonia fourcadei*
Nov (1,2 m)
The long narrow
leaves of this plant
form a fan around its
base, and the
flower-stem
bears white or
pink flowers.
Growing on
mountain
foothills, the
flowers are
particularly
abundant when
good rain
follows a
bush-fire.

◀ Candelabra Flower ▼
*Brunsvigia orientalis*
Feb - Apr (50 - 80 cm)
A single stalk grows up from the
sandy soil, ending in a large cluster
(about 40 cm across) of crimson
flowers. The flower-head becomes
papery when it dries, and it breaks
off and rolls in the wind dispersing
seeds. The leaves, which grow
from the bulb after the
flowers die, lie almost
flat on the ground.

*Dried
flowerhead*

# FYNBOS

## HERBAL AND MEDICINAL

Plants have been harvested for their valuable medicinal and herbal properties from the earliest times. Today, there is growing interest in rediscovering and identifying new health products from fynbos plants. The plants, however, need to be harvested wisely, to prevent over-exploitation and loss of biodiversity.

**▲ Carpet Geranium ►**
*Geranium incanum*
Sep - Jan (up to 30 cm)
Low-growing, this plant has fine leaves and grows in large patches on road verges, like a carpet. The flowers vary from pale-pink to purple. An infusion made from this plant is used to treat venerea diseases, menstruation problems and bladder infectio

**Rose-scented Pelargonium ►**
*Pelargonium capitatum*
Sep - Jan (30 - 90 cm)
This low bush has straggly branches and velvety, crinkly leaves with small pink to purple flowers. Apart from the flowers, the plant is covered with long, soft, white hairs. If crushed it has a pleasant smell, and is one of the species cultivated for geranium oil. Rubbed onto skin, the leaves soothe scratches and calouses.

**Ivy-leafed Pelargonium ►**
*Pelargonium peltatum*
Oct - Jan (climber)
Climbing over shrubs and trees, the leaves of this creeper resemble an ivy leaf and are fleshy and glossy. The sour-tasting leaves are used to soothe sore throats, and when pounded, can be made into a useful antiseptic for skin abrasions and minor burns. The flowers grow at the end of short stalks, and are pink to mauve with darker markings on the upper two petals.

**◄ Sorrel**
*Oxalis purpurea* Apr - Sep (3 cm)
The flowers of the Sorrel are deep purplish-red with yellow centres. The leaves are broad, heart-shaped and arranged in threes, like clovers. Early in the 17th Century, it was discovered that eating Sorrel leaves was very beneficial to sailors suffering from scurvy.

**▼ Honeybee ►**
*Apis mellifera* (15 mm)
These bees feed on nectar and pollen which they carry in pollen sacs on their hind legs. They live in social colony with a single queen bee. They make 'honeycomb' nests.

**◄ Minaret Flower (Wildedagga) ▼**
*Leonotis leonurus* Mar - Jul (2 m)
Although commonly called 'wild dagga', because of its strong-smelling leaves, it has no narcotic properties. The plant is nevertheless traditionally used for the treatment of skin disorders and snake bite, and for headaches and coughs. This tall shrub has 'box-like' stems and orange-red, velvety flowers. The narrow leaves are paired and rough, and it grows on dune-scrub and open mountain slopes.

D
flower-h

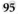

### ◄ Dune Salvia (Wild Sage)
*Salvia aurea*
May - Jan
(1 m)
Dune Salvia can be very bushy, and has soft, silvery-grey, strong-smelling leaves. The flowers are yellowish-brown. The greenish-purple seed-pockets stay on the plant long after the flowers have died. The leaves may be used in cooking as a substitute for the herb sage.

### Septemberbossie ▼
*Polygala myrtifolia*
May - Dec (2,5 m)
This wide bush grows in a variety of habitats. It has narrow, leathery, shiny, green leaves with large, mauve to purple-pink flowers resembling butterflies. Muslims used to boil the bark, and use the water to wash their dead. The leaves were used as a poultice to relieve the pain of gout.

### Blombos ►
*Metalasia muricata*
Jan - Dec (2 m)
Blombos is a widespread, variable shrub that grows from sea level to high altitudes. It is traditionally used to make a refreshing cup of tea.

### Carpenter Bee ►
Family Xylocopinae
(10 - 35 mm)
Carpenter bees build nests in dry wood, including dead trees, stems of a dead Aloe, or dry timber in buildings.

### ◄ Mountain Buchu
*Agathosma ciliaris* Jun - Nov (up to 40 cm)
Very abundant from Still Bay to Mossel Bay, the Mountain Buchu is found on granite or sandstone ridges. As with all buchus it releases a strong-smelling oil, particularly when the leaves are crushed, and it makes a good addition to potpourris. Several species of this family form the basis of a small buchu-oil industry.

### ▼ Buchu
*Agathosma capensis* Aug - Apr (0,5 - 1,5 m)
Buchus are woody members of the citrus family, growing on sunny mountain slopes and in coastal scrub. The round clusters of small flowers vary in colour from white, pink, mauve to bluish-purple. The lower stems are woody, whilst the upper parts are surrounded by tiny, very strong-smelling leaves. When crushed they release oils that are used to flavour ice-cream, jam and cooldrinks, and are also added to perfumes. Extracts of the plant are used to treat indigestion and hangovers.

### Stone Buchu ►
*Coleonema album*
Jul - Nov (0,5 - 2 m)
Found close to the sea, especially in the Robberg area, the Stone Buchu is common among rocks and on ledges. This evergreen, woody shrub is a useful garden plant as it forms an attractive backdrop, even without the flowers. The tiny oil-glands on the surface of leaves, fruits and petals, release an aromatic oil used for making perfumes and diuretic medicines.

# DUNE AND ESTUARIES

Life isn't easy for dune and estuarine plants. Dune plants have to cope with salty spray from the sea, sandy soils that dry out quickly, and constantly shifting sand. Some plants adapt by having thick, fleshy, tough leaves which store water, while others have no leaves at all. Plants living around estuaries have high levels of salt in the mud and sand. Reeds and sedges, which often grow in dense bands, are well suited to this.

## TREES AND BUSHES

Woody vegetation lines the banks of estuaries providing perches for water birds, such as cormorants and kingfishers. Amongst the dunes, bush clumps and thickets provide shelter to shy antelope, such as duiker and grysbok. Invasive Australian Acacias are rapidly replacing the native dune vegetation, and drastically changing the ecology of the dunes.

*Many plants grow close to the ground, stabilising the sand and allowing others to gain a hold. Dunes are fragile eco-systems and very sensitive to trampling.*

### ◀ White Milkwood ▼
*Sideroxylon inerme*
Jan - Jul (10 m) 579
Evergreen
These small trees, often with twisted barks, form dense thickets in coastal areas and dry forests. The leaves are leathery, dark-green above and paler below; the flowers are green-white; the bark and purple-black berries contain a milky fluid. The 'Post Office Tree' in Mossel Bay is a national monument (see page 133), and all White Milkwoods are protected by law.

### ◀ Cross-berry Raisin ▼
*Grewia occidentalis*
Aug - Mar (6 m) 463
Evergreen
This shrub has pale-grey, smooth bark, light-green leaves and star-shaped, pink-mauve flowers. It grows in coastal forest and shrub. It has four-lobed, square, yellow-orange fruit which is brownish-red when ripe. The bark, soaked in hot water, is said to heal wounds.

### ▼ Narrow-leaved Camphor-bush (Wild Camphor Bush)
*Tarchonanthus camphoratus*
Mar - May (9 m) 733
Evergreen
A small tree with leathery leaves that are grey-green above and cream-coloured below. When crushed they smell of camphor. Both the cream-white flowers and the seeds are covered with white hairs. It grows in dune-scrub and at the edge of forests.

### Dune Guarri (Sea Guarri) ▼
*Euclea racemosa*
Dec - Mar (6 m) 599
Evergreen
The bark of this small tree is smooth and grey, and its leaves are thick and leathery, paler green below than above. It has small cream-white flowers and black berries, and grows in coastal forest and dune-scrub.

**◄ Krantz Aloe**
*Aloe arborescens*
Apr - Jul
(2 - 3 m)
Each branch bears a rosette of curved prickly leaves from which 4 - 5 flowering stems grow. Clusters of orange or scarlet flowers form a cone shape at the top of each stem. It grows in rocky mountain passes and on coastal cliffs and dunes.

**Bushtick-berry ►**
**(Bietou)**
*Chrysanthemoides monilifera*
May - Sep
(2 m) 736.1
Evergreen
This shrub has leathery, grey-green, glossy leaves which are covered with white, cobweb-like hairs when young. Its flowers are bright-yellow and daisy-like. Birds love to eat the black-purple berries.

**Waxy Kuni-rhus (Glossy Currant Bush) ▼**
*Rhus lucida* Aug - Oct
(3 - 4 m) 388.1 Evergreen
This small tree has shiny, leathery leaves, small, cream-white flowers, and small, shiny brown berries. The hard, tough wood is good for fence posts.

**Horsefly ►**
Family
Tabanidae
(10 - 25 mm)
Horseflies feed on nectar and pollen. The females have piercing mouth parts and also suck blood. The larvae feed on small insects, tadpoles or worms.

**▼ Blue-fruit Currant-rhus**
**(Dune Crow-berry)** *Rhus crenata*
Feb - Mar (2 m) 380.1 Evergreen
With a strong but pleasant scent, the thin, leathery leaves are dark grey-green above and yellow-green below. It has small, white-cream flowers in the autumn and black berries in the winter.

**◄ Candleberry (Waxberry)**
*Myrica cordifolia*
Jun - Oct (up to 2 m) Evergreen
The Candleberry has small bluish berries, covered with white waxy scales which the early Cape settlers used for making candles and soap. The plant has long underground stems from which many new plants grow.

**Coast Olive ►**
**(Dune Olive)**
*Olea exasperata*
Nov - Feb
(1 - 7 m) 619
Evergreen
This shrub has leathery, paired leaves, and clusters of white flowers grow at the tips of leafless twigs. Its oval fruit is purple-black. In the past the root was used as an antidote for snake-bites.

# DUNE AND ESTUARIES

## LOW LYING PLANTS

The low-lying plants are those that creep over the surface of the sand-dunes and never grow very high. They help to stabilise the dunes, and to prevent excessive wind erosion and movement of sand. These plants have shallow root-systems, and are able to use any surface water, before it drains away into the sand.

◄ **Sea Lavender** ►
*Limonium scabrum*
Jul - Jan (30 cm)
This plant has a rosette of blue-green leaves at its base, and branched stems with many pale-mauve, papery flowers.

▼ **Oranjegousblo**
*Gazania krebsiana* Aug - Nov (20 cr
Low-growing, without a proper stem and wi variable-shaped leaves, this plant has yello orange flowers which may be up to 5 cm wi
It grows in dry grassland and along the edge of roads.

◄ **Seeplakkie** ▲
*Scaevola plumieri*
Nov - Apr (45 cm)
This is a creeping plant with woody stems and white flowers that grow in clusters from the base of the large, leathery leaves. It grows on sandy shores just above the high-tide level and stabilises shifting sand-dunes.

**Sea Pumpkin** ▼
*Arctotheca populifolia*
Sep - May (30 cm)
The thick, rounded leaves are covered with silvery hairs, and its yellow flowers have 'petals' which are indented at the tip. It grows at river mouths and on coastal sand dunes.

◄ **Sour Fig** ►
*Carpobrotus deliciosus*
Aug - Oct (creeper)
The long branches, with thick, fleshy leaves trail along the ground with roots anchoring them to the sand at various points. The flowers are large, satiny-purple with yellow centres. The ripe fruit is sweet and juicy.

◄ **Pigs Ear** ▼
*Cotyledon orbiculata*
Flowering (1 m)
The leaves of this poisonous plant are thick, fleshy and grey-green with purple-red tinged edges. The waxy flowers on long stems may be orange, pink or red.

*Dried flower-heads*

▲ **Soutbo**
*Chenolea diffusa* Jan - Feb (10
Growing low on the ground, it is a stragg red-stemmed plant with silver-grey le which become orange or red. It has very yellow flowers. It grows on rocks, banks ar sand at the edge of coastal rivers and lago

▲ **Wild Cineraria**
*Senecio elegans* Aug - Mar (60 cm)
This plant has purple flowers with yellow centres.
Its leaves are finely notched, and are thinner and
juicier on plants growing near the sea.

▼**Bulrush** ►
*Typha latifolia capensis*
Dec - Mar/Jul - Sep
(2 m)
Amongst the long,
narrow leaves of
this plant are tall
stems with spikes
of flowers. The yellow,
male flowers, on the upper
part of the spike, fall off after
pollination leaving the brown
'bulrush' of female flowers. It
grows in marshy ground.

**Christmas Berry** ►
*Chironia baccifera*
Sep - Mar (45 cm)
This little shrub, with
small, narrow leaves, forms
a round bush with brilliant
pink flowers, followed by
bright orange-red berries.
It grows on coastal sand
dunes and on sunny
mountain slopes.

▼ **Dune Slack
Rush** ►
*Juncus kraussii*
Dec - Jan
(1 - 1,5 m)
This is one of several sedge
species which borders
estuaries in the Garden
Route area.

◄ **Reeds** ►
*Phragmites australis*
Dec - Jun
(0,6 - 4 m)
The flowering stems
of this reed are
feathery, and it grows
in wet places such as
river beds.

**Coastal Buffalo Grass**
*Strenotaphrum secundatum* (up to 20 cm)
Prefering sandy soils near the sea or fresh water
sources, it is commonly used for golf-course lawns.

**Glasswort Samphire** ▼
*Sarcocornia perennis*
(30 mm)
A sprawling perennial
succulent, it forms mats on
estuarine mudflats, and is
submerged at high tide.

◄ **Dune Ehrharta** ►
*Ehrharta villosa*
Oct - Apr (90 cm)
This grass grows in
shady moist places,
often at forest edges.

# LAND MAMMALS

The diversity and abundance of mammal species increases from the coastline inland. This is because of the changes in vegetation and availability of suitable habitats. Each animal favours specific types of habitat. Some are able to live across a wide range of habitats, like the bushpig, while others can only live in specific habitat types, such as the Cape Clawless Otter. Many of the mammals share habitats, but each has its own lifestyle. Some are arboreal (moving above the ground), like the Vervet Monkey (but they also spend time foraging on the ground); others are fossorial (living in burrows), like the Cape Dune Molerat; while others are entirely terrestrial (living on the ground), like the antelope.

The numbers of mammal species in the southern Cape has declined or disappeared because of hunting, the development of towns and farms, and other human activities. Today, only two elephants, an old female and a young bull, roam the Knysna Forest (page 133).

*Mammals are measured in height H - ground to shoulder, or in length L - tip of nose to tip of tail.*

*The solitary Cape Clawless Otter sunning itself on a river bank*

# Mammals

Mammals occupy different feeding niches. They may be carnivores (meat-eaters), herbivores (plant-eaters), insectivores (insect-eaters), frugivores (fruit-eaters) or omnivores (a mix of different diets). The herbivores include browsers, (animals that eat leaves, stems and seeds) and grazers (those that prefer grasses), and therefore make use of different parts of the vegetation. The Cape Grysbok and Common and Blue Duiker are nocturnal (active during the night), but have been illustrated here with the other antelope.

*It is illegal to hunt animals without a permit. Animal numbers are already threatened by loss of habitat, therefore limits are set on when and where hunting can take place. Please respect our wildlife.*

▲ **Vervet Monkey**
*Cercopithecus aethiops*
(L: M 1 - 1,3 m; F 1 m)
Vervet Monkeys are found in riverine woodlands, in troops of up to twenty. They sleep in tall trees and forage during the day, on the ground and in trees, searching for wild fruit, birds, eggs and insects.

◀ **Chacma Baboon**
*Papio ursinus*
(L: M 1,2 - 1,6 m; F 1 - 1,2 m)
Baboons prefer mountains, hills and forests with tall trees or rocky cliffs for shelter. They live in troops of 20 - 100 individuals, and forage during the day for a wide range of food, including fruit, leaves, flowers, insects, mice, birds and even young antelope.

▼ **Small and Large Grey Mongoose**
*Galerella pulverulenta / Herpestes ichneumon*
(L: 55 - 69 cm / 1 m)
The Small Grey Mongoose depicted here, lives in a variety of habitats, from forest to open scrub, eating insects, mice and birds. Its legs are darker than the rest of its body. The Large Grey Mongoose has a black tail-tip, long hair around the back legs, and eats small animals, even Puff Adders.

**Dassie** ▶ ▼
(Rock Hyrax)
*Procavia capensis*
(L: 45 - 60 cm)
Dassies live in groups and like to sunbathe on rocky outcrops with one member of the group standing guard for predators, such as Black Eagles. They also climb trees. Dassies eat grass, leaves, fruit and bark. Their closest relative is the elephant (page 133)!

▼ **Cape Dune Molerat**
*Bathyergus suillus* (L: M 33 cm; F 30 cm)
The body of these molerats is light-brown. They live underground in sandy soil where they feed on roots and bulbs.

**Bontebok ►**
*Damaliscus dorcas dorcas*
(H: 90 cm)
These rare antelope are only found in a small coastal plain region with fynbos vegetation in the southern Cape. They prefer areas with short grass, near water sources, and they graze in the morning and late afternoon. Both males and females have horns.

*(M)*

**▲ Southern Cape Bushbuck**
*Tragelaphus scriptus* (H: M 80 cm; F 70 cm)
These timid, medium-sized antelope live near water, from coastal dune bush to mountain forests. They are usually seen alone and feed mostly at night, browsing on a variety of plants. Only males have horns.

**Blue Duiker ►**
*Philantomba monticola*
(H: M 30 cm; F 32 cm)
Blue Duiker is the smallest southern African antelope. The upperparts vary from slate-grey to dark-brown with a grey-blue sheen, and underparts are white. Living in dense forests and bush near water sources, they eat mainly fallen leaves, fruit and flowers, and often follow troops of monkeys, eating the food that is dropped from the trees. Both males and females have horns.

**Dung Beetle ▼**
Subfamily *Scarabaeinae*
Insect (5 - 50 mm)
Dung Beetles vary in colour. They feed on the dung of plant-eating mammals. Most species roll dung into balls and bury them for later use. They are strong flyers although rather clumsy.

**◄ Common Duiker**
*Sylvicapra grimmia*
(H: M 50 cm; F 70 cm)
Common Duikers prefer scrub and bush-covered country. They are found in undergrowth and thickets browsing on leaves, fruit, flowers and seeds. They also dig for tubers and roots. Only the males have horns.

*(M)*

**▲ Rhinoceros Beetle**
*Oryctes boas*
Insect (30 mm)
The male beetles have a horn which they use in fights with other males. The larvae, large white grubs, are often found in rotting vegetation or animal dung.

**Cape Grysbok ►**
*Raphicerus melanotis* (H: 54 cm)
Active mainly at night, these animals are found on their own or in pairs. They live in fairly thick scrub-bush in fynbos. Grysbok are selective feeders, foraging for palatable grasses, herbs, leaves, fruit and pods. Only the males have horns.

*(M)*

# MAINLY NOCTURNAL

**M**ammals are active at different times. Those illustrated here are mainly nocturnal (active during the night). They often fill the same or similar niches as the diurnal (day) animals but use them at night. They are well adapted to a nocturnal lifestyle. Some have very large eyes to capture as much light as possible, while others compensate with excellent hearing and/or smell.

*These mammals are often common, but infrequently seen because of their nocturnal habits. A spotlight is the best way of sighting these creatures as their shining eyes can easily be spotted in the dark.*

### ▲ Leopard
*Panthera pardus*
(H: 60 - 75 cm)
Once widespread, these shy animals are now very rare. They live alone, mainly in mountainous, rugged areas. Active at night, they hunt mice, dassies, bushpigs and medium-sized antelope. They often hide their prey from other predators by hauling it up trees or dragging it under bushes.

### Cape Hare ▶
*Lepus capensis* (L: 45 - 60 cm)
Cape Hares prefer dry, open grassland areas. They eat plants and get moisture from their food and the dew. Although active at night, they may also be seen in the early morning or late afternoon, usually on their own.

### ▲ Cape Serotine Bat
*Eptesicus capensis* (L: 8,5 cm)
These bats are high fliers and they eat insects. They gather in small numbers in rock crevices, roofs or trees.

### Vlei Rat ▶
*Otomys irroratus* (L: 24 cm)
Vlei Rats are seen during the day in marshy areas or damp grasslands. They eat shoots and stems of grass, sedges, reeds and other plants. Their saucer-shaped nests are built on dry, raised ground or in clumps of grass.

### ▲ Egyptian Fruit Bat
*Rousettus aegyptiacus*
(L: 15 cm)
Living in forests and riverine woodlands, these bats often shelter in caves or old mine-shafts. They eat ripe fruit.

### Striped Mouse ▶
*Rhabdomys pumilio* (L: 18 - 21 cm)
Striped Mice live in grassy areas. They eat insects, seeds and other plant material, including the fleshy parts of Protea flowers which they help to pollinate. They are the most common mice found in the fynbos region, and are an important food source for many predators. They dig long, chambered burrows or build round nests in clumps of grass.

◀ **Caracal**
*Felis caracal*
(H: 40 - 45 cm)
Caracals occur throughout the southern Cape, from fynbos to forest. They are nocturnal, solitary and secretive, hunting mainly birds and small- to medium-sized mammals. Their fur colour varies according to region.

▲ **Small- and Large-spotted Genet**
*Genetta genetta / Genetta tigrina*
(L: 85 - 100 cm)
Genets usually hunt at night and feed on insects, mice, frogs and birds. The Small-spotted Genet has white facial markings and a white tail-tip. The Large-spotted Genet has a black tail-tip.

**Cape Clawless Otter** ▶
*Aonyx capensis*
(L: 1 - 1,3 m)
hese solitary otters swim in both fresh and sea water. They dive in search of frogs, crabs, fish, octopus and also eat insects, birds and reptiles.

**Cape Porcupine** ▼
*Hystrix africaeaustralis* (L: 84 - 86 cm)
They are the largest southern African rodents. Living in a variety of habitats, usually alone, they are mainly active at night, often spending the day in caves or burrows. They dig for tubers, bulbs and roots but also eat fruit and gnaw bark off trees.

▲ **Water Mongoose**
*Atilax paludinosus* (L: 80 - 100 cm)
Living near shallow water, these mongooses dig in the mud to find crabs and mussels, which they throw onto the rocks to break their shells. They also eat frogs, rodents, birds, fish and insects.

◀ **Bushpig**
*Potamochoerus porcus*
(H: M 76 cm; F 65 cm)
Active at night, these animals live in groups of 7 - 12, in forests, bush or reed-beds, near water. They dig for plant bulbs and tubers with their snouts, and also eat earthworms, insects, fruit and carrion.

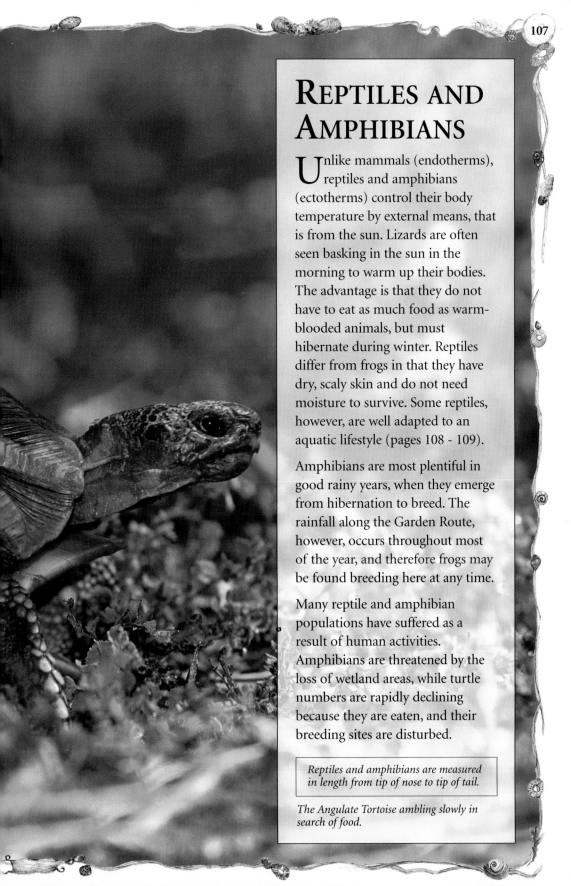

# REPTILES AND AMPHIBIANS

Unlike mammals (endotherms), reptiles and amphibians (ectotherms) control their body temperature by external means, that is from the sun. Lizards are often seen basking in the sun in the morning to warm up their bodies. The advantage is that they do not have to eat as much food as warm-blooded animals, but must hibernate during winter. Reptiles differ from frogs in that they have dry, scaly skin and do not need moisture to survive. Some reptiles, however, are well adapted to an aquatic lifestyle (pages 108 - 109).

Amphibians are most plentiful in good rainy years, when they emerge from hibernation to breed. The rainfall along the Garden Route, however, occurs throughout most of the year, and therefore frogs may be found breeding here at any time.

Many reptile and amphibian populations have suffered as a result of human activities. Amphibians are threatened by the loss of wetland areas, while turtle numbers are rapidly declining because they are eaten, and their breeding sites are disturbed.

*Reptiles and amphibians are measured in length from tip of nose to tip of tail.*

*The Angulate Tortoise ambling slowly in search of food.*

# WATERBASED

The amphibians (frogs and toads) and some reptiles are adapted to a water-based environment. Amphibians, although not always dependent on standing bodies of water, need moist (fresh water) habitats to live and breed. Their slimy, porous skin does not prevent water loss, and they will dry out from lack of moisture. The two turtle species and the sea snake are marine reptiles, well adapted to sea life, with salt secreting glands to rid the body of excess salt.

*Toads differ from frogs in having dry, rough skin, which excretes a white mucus when threatened. The statement that "toads give you warts" is an old wives' tale.*

**▲ Common Brown Water Snake**
*Lycodonomorphus rufulus*
(60 - 87 cm)
These harmless snakes are olive to brown, with light pink-yellow bellies and lips, living near rivers and streams. At night, they hunt frogs, tadpoles and fish, squeezing the prey before swallowing it.

**◄ Yellow-bellied Sea Snake**
*Pelamis platurus* (0,6 - 1 m)
Living in tropical seas, these poisonous snakes feed on small fish. Their flat, bar-like tails are good for swimming.

**◄ Loggerhead Turtle**
*Caretta caretta* (1,5 m)
Loggerhead Turtles drift in the deep sea when young, feeding on floating animals. When older, they move closer to shore and feed on crabs, sea urchins and molluscs.

**Leatherback Turtle ▼**
*Dermochelys coriacea*
(2,5 - 3 m)
These rare turtles are the heaviest living reptiles. They have clawless flippers for swimming, and eat jellyfish and bluebottles. They live out at sea and usually return to the same beaches to lay their eggs.

◄ **Clicking Stream Frog** ►
*Strongylopus grayii*
(4,5 - 6 cm)
The repeated, short, sharp
alls of these frogs can be heard
hroughout the year even in winter.
ggs are laid in a capsule of stiff jelly.

**► Arum Lily Frog ►**
*Hyperolius horstockii*
(3,5 cm)
These frogs are found in
reeds, often far from
water, and in the flowers
of Arum Lilies where they
become whitish in colour.
They have suckers on all
their toes and fingers.

◄ **Banded
Stream Frog**
*Strongylopus bonaspei*
(4 cm)
The Banded
Stream Frog
prefers marshy ground
and seepage areas of mountain
streams. It has brown-orange stripes
on its back, a pointed snout and very
long toes. It is an exceptionally good
jumper, and can cover two metres in a
single leap. The 'plops' you hear as
you stroll along a river bank are most
likely made by these frogs.

**▼ Cape River Frog**
*Rana fuscigula* (7,5 cm; up to 12 cm)
A large, common frog, the Cape River Frog is
usually detected when it 'plops' into nearby water
for safety. Males, calling from deep water support
themselves on floating vegetation in permanent
ponds, streams and rivers. They have webbed
hind toes because they
are more aquatic
than terrestrial.

**Cape Sand Frog ▼**
*Tomopterna delalandei* (up to 5 cm)
Although restricted to fresh water for breeding,
the Cape Sand Frog also forages on sandy
beaches for small invertebrates. It occurs in open
sand and grassland habitats and has
a prominent 'spade' on its heel for
digging backwards into the sandy
soil when preparing to hibernate.

◄ **Common Caco**
*Cacosternum boettgeri* (2,3 cm)
The Common Caco favours any
marshy wetlands and swamp grasslands where
the water is shallow. It calls from the base of
vegetation in high-pitched clicks, day and
night. Cacos hide for most of the year but are
very abundant after good rains.

**Common Platanna ▼**
*Xenopus laevis* (7 cm)
They are aquatic frogs that
breed and feed underwater,
eating insects and snails,
as well as small
animals and
nestlings that fall
into the water. Breeding
is from early spring to late
summer. The eggs are
attached to submerged
grass, stones
and sticks.

◄ ▼ **Raucous Toad**
*Bufo rangeri*
(up to 10 cm)
As its name
implies, the Raucous
Toad has a very loud,
rasping *'kwaak, kwaak'*. It calls from
exposed areas near the water or from
rocks in shallow water. It is
found in open and bush
areas, and is also
common in gardens.
Different colour
variations are
found.

*ling*

*Common
Platanna
tadpoles*

# LANDBASED

Reptiles can live away from water because of their dry, horny skin, and have successfully inhabited most environments. Most of these reptiles are generalists, occurring in a wide range of habitat types. They do, however, require shelter, such as rocks or scrub, for hibernating and resting, and will therefore seldom be found along the beaches. The Southern Rock Agama, however, may be found foraging amongst washed-up debris along the high watermark.

*The vast majority of our snakes, and all our lizards, are not poisonous, and are therefore totally harmless. Like most animals, the few dangerous snakes only harm when threatened.*

**Angulate Tortoise ►**
*Chersina angulata*
(16 - 26 cm)
Angulate Tortoises feed mostly on grasses and other plants, and at shallow pools, drinking water through their noses.

**◄ Common Padloper**
*Homopus areolatus*
(12 cm)
They are found in the moister coastal regions, often sheltering under rocks or in disu animal burrows. The female lays 2 eggs in a small nest hole in shady soi They can live up to 30 years in captivity.

**◄ Knysna Dwarf Chameleon**
*Bradypodion damaranum*
(12 - 18 cm)
These small reptiles blend into the trees and bushes where they live in wet coastal areas. They feed on insects at night.

**◄ Marble Leaf-toed Gecko ▼**
*Phyllodactylus porphyreus*
(8 - 10 cm)
Active at night, these geckos often feed on insects around outside lights. When provoked, geckos may click, chirp and squeal.

**Cape Skink ►**
*Mabuya capensis*
(20 - 27 cm)
Cape Skinks feed mainly on insects such as grasshoppers and beetles. They live in tunnels which they dig in loose soil.

(M)

**◄ Southern Rock Agama ►**
*Agama atra*
(20 - 32 cm)
Often seen basking on rocky outcrops, these lizards eat ants and termites. The male lizards bob their heads to warn off intruders, or possibly to attract females.

**Plain Rain Frog**
*Breviceps fuscus* (5 cm)
These frogs are found in coastal mountains from Knysna to Swellendam. They live in shallow tunnels up to 15 cm deep, or on the forest floor in moist, shady spots. Their loud chirruping call, which is repeated at short intervals, sounds like a police whistle.

(F)

**▼ Cape Cobra**
*Naja nivea*
(1,2 - 1,7 m)
When disturbed, these very
poisonous snakes raise their
bodies and spread a 'hood'
just below the head. Colour
varies from yellow to
reddish-brown, even
black. In the day they
hunt rats, mice, lizards,
frogs and other snakes.

**Boomslang ▲**
*Dispholidus typus*
(1,2 - 2 m)
Also called 'tree-snakes', these
very poisonous reptiles live
mainly in trees. During the day
they hunt chameleons, lizards
and young birds.

**Puff Adder ►**
*Bitis arietans* (0,7 - 2 m)
Puff Adders are very poisonous, slow-moving
snakes. They often bask in the sun in grass
or bush, or across footpaths. They eat
mainly rats and mice.

**Olive House Snake ▼**
*Lamprophis inornatus* (0,6 - 1,3 m)
Found mostly in damp places, these harmless
snakes eat rats, mice, frogs and sometimes
other snakes.

**▼ Common Slug-eater**
*Duberria lutrix* (30 - 43 cm)
Living in damp places, these harmless
snakes eat snails and
slugs. When alarmed
they roll up into a
spiral.

**▲ Common or Rhombic Egg-eater**
*Dasypeltis scabra* (0,5 - 11,6 m)
When threatened, these harmless snakes coil
up and rub their scales against one another
to make a loud hissing noise. They only eat
birds' eggs, which they swallow whole.

# BIRD LIFE

There is a rich diversity of bird species occurring along the Garden Route because of the wide range of habitats. Birds require specific habitat conditions that will provide them with the rich food supply needed for survival, and also the sheltered sites for nesting and breeding. Some birds occur only in one type of habitat, like some of the Cape fynbos species; others range across a wide variety of habitats, like the Hadeda Ibis. Endemic birds (usually originating in the area) are very vulnerable to habitat loss, as their feeding and breeding needs are so specific.

Bird watching is a great hobby for people of all ages. Knowing distribution and habitat preferences is the first step in identification. The next step is recognising the different bill shapes and body proportions of the different bird groups. To save hours of frustrating peering into thick vegetation, try enticing the birds out by 'spishing'. This is a series of short, loud sounds made through one's teeth sounding like a tire deflating in quiet bursts. It is a recognised way of persuading the small and inconspicuous species to reveal themselves.

*Birds are numbered with the Roberts number; and their sizes are given from beak-tip to tail-tip.*

*This solitary Hamerkop waits patiently for a frog meal by a slow-moving river.*

# WATERBIRDS

Water birds are associated with a wide range of aquatic habitats. These range from salt to fresh water, and from small, temporary pools to large, permanent water bodies. The birds each have a specific niche within this environment. To forage and breed, birds use the banks of water bodies, the water surface itself, deep water and the vegetation on, or surrounding, the water.

## SEA AND ROCKY CLIFF BIRDS

Birds that have a close relationship with the seashore have some interesting adaptations that help them cope with their environment. Primarily many are well adapted for swimming. Some of the genuine sea birds, like the Cape Gannet, the Jackass Penguin and the African Black Oystercatcher eat marine animals, and cannot avoid taking in sea water. They have a special adrenal gland that excretes excess salt.

*Please don't litter. Littering has a detrimental effect on many water birds, and can cause terrible maiming and often a very slow death. If items such as plastic or string are found lying around water bodies, pick them up and put them in a dustbin.*

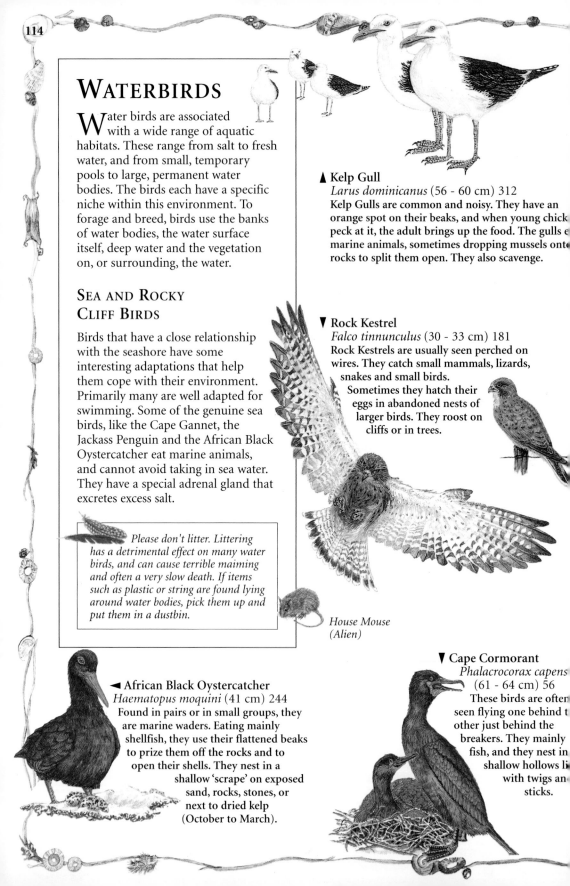

**▲ Kelp Gull**
*Larus dominicanus* (56 - 60 cm) 312
Kelp Gulls are common and noisy. They have an orange spot on their beaks, and when young chick peck at it, the adult brings up the food. The gulls e marine animals, sometimes dropping mussels onto rocks to split them open. They also scavenge.

**▼ Rock Kestrel**
*Falco tinnunculus* (30 - 33 cm) 181
Rock Kestrels are usually seen perched on wires. They catch small mammals, lizards, snakes and small birds.
Sometimes they hatch their eggs in abandoned nests of larger birds. They roost on cliffs or in trees.

House Mouse
(Alien)

**◄ African Black Oystercatcher**
*Haematopus moquini* (41 cm) 244
Found in pairs or in small groups, they are marine waders. Eating mainly shellfish, they use their flattened beaks to prize them off the rocks and to open their shells. They nest in a shallow 'scrape' on exposed sand, rocks, stones, or next to dried kelp (October to March).

**▼ Cape Cormorant**
*Phalacrocorax capens*
(61 - 64 cm) 56
These birds are often seen flying one behind t other just behind the breakers. They mainly fish, and they nest in shallow hollows li with twigs an sticks.

▲ Cape Gannet
*Morus capensis* (84 - 94 cm) 53
These large white birds, with pointed black tails and wing tips, gather at sea in large flocks and follow shoals of fish. They breed only on selected islands. They can be seen plunging into the sea from heights of up to 10 metres, throwing up a fountain of spray.

◄ Swift Tern ►
*Sterna bergii* (46 - 50 cm) (324)
This large tern is found along the coast, where it hunts for fish near the water surface and roosts on beaches.
Its large size and yellow bill are diagnostic. It occurs in gregarious flocks, often with other seabirds such as gulls and other terns.

◄ White-breasted Cormorant
*Phalacrocorax carbo* (90 cm) 55
These birds often perch on a branch or log to dry their outstretched wings. They eat mainly fish and they nest on ledges. They may also be found inland.

▼ White-fronted Plover
*Charadrius marginatus* (18 cm) 246
The White-fronted Plover is usually first spotted running along the shoreline looking for insects. It may also be seen up along the dunes amongst the low-lying vegetation and debris where it nests. It is a very small, squat-looking bird, usually spotted in pairs.

Jackass Penguin ►
*Spheniscus demersus* (60 cm) 3
Occuring only in southern Africa, these flightless birds make a sound like braying donkeys. They feed mainly on pilchards. Pollution, over-fishing and egg-collection have caused a serious drop in numbers.

# WATERBIRDS

## ESTUARIES AND FRESHWATER

The many dams, pans and vleis of the area provide ideal places to see a variety of birds.

Whether they are scavengers or hunters, or eat plants, each has a specialist role to play in the eco-chains. At estuaries the salt waters of the sea meet the nutrient-rich sediments washed down by the rivers. These sediments accumulate as thick mud flats around the river mouths. Many types of shellfish (pages 76 - 77) living in this rich mud, provide food for birds, especially waders.

◄ **Fish Eagle** ►
*Haliaeetus vocifer*
(63 - 73 cm) 148
Fish Eagles have a magnificent call. They hunt fish from a perch, making a shallow dive to catch the fish in their claws. Fish Eagles build their nests in trees.

*Flathead Mullet (page 73)*

(F)

(M)

◄ **Pied Kingfisher**
*Ceryle rudis*
(25 - 29 cm) 428
These black-and-white birds are usually found in pairs. They are often seen hovering above water looking for fish, but also eat shellfish and insects. They nest in holes in banks.

**Reed Cormorant** ▼
*Phalacrocorax africanus*
(60 cm) 58
The most common of the cormorants, these birds have yellow beaks and long tails. They are often seen with wings stretched out to dry. They eat fish, frogs and aquatic insects.

**Giant Kingfisher** ▼
*Ceryle maxima*
(43 - 46 cm) 429
With speckled black-and-white backs, these are the largest kingfishers. They eat crabs, fish and frogs and nest in holes in streams or river banks.

(M)

**Malachite Kingfisher** ►
*Alcedo cristata* (14 cm) 431
This small jewel of a bird is always found near water, usually in pairs. They hunt small fish and tadpoles and nest in holes in a bank.

### Egyptian Goose ▼
*Alopochen aegyptiacus*
(63 - 73 cm) 102

These birds look similar to the South African Shelduck. Their call is a rapid honking made before take-off and sometimes during flight. They eat aquatic plants, grass and seedlings.

### Yellow-billed Duck ►
*Anas undulata*
(51 - 63 cm) 104

The bright yellow bill, with a central black patch, are diagnostic features of Yellow-billed Ducks. They are found in pairs and flocks mostly on both open freshwater but also in estuaries. They feed on plant matter, bottoms-up in deep water, or by grazing on land.

### Moorhen ▼
*Gallinula chloropus*
(30 - 36 cm)
226

The Moorhen is common around many freshwater bodies. It is mostly seen swimming on open water, but also feeds in adjacent wet grasslands. It is very distinctive with its black body, bright red forehead and bill with a yellow tip.

### ◄ Dragonfly
Suborder
*Anisoptera*
Insect
(wingspan 45 - 140 mm)

These insects can fly up to 80 km per hour! They hunt whilst flying, catching other flying insects and are often seen skimming low over water.

### ▼ Red-knobbed Coot
*Fulica cristata* (43 cm) 228

Coots are seen in pairs or large flocks. They feed by dipping under water to pull up aquatic plants. The two red knobs on their heads become larger when the birds breed.

### ▼ Dabchick
*Tachybaptus ruficollis* (20 cm) 8

When moving fast, Dabchicks look like they are running on the water. They eat a variety of aquatic animals. Their nests are floating platforms made of weeds.

### ▲ Darter
*Anhinga melanogaster* (79 cm) 60

Darters have slender 'kinked' necks and are also known as 'snakebirds'. They hunt fish underwater, impaling them with their dagger-like beaks. They also catch frogs.

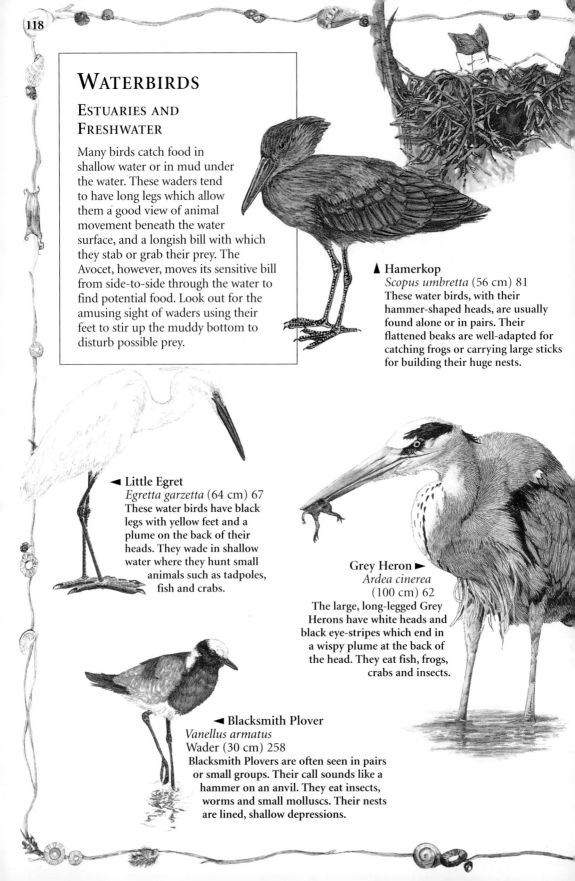

# WATERBIRDS

## ESTUARIES AND FRESHWATER

Many birds catch food in shallow water or in mud under the water. These waders tend to have long legs which allow them a good view of animal movement beneath the water surface, and a longish bill with which they stab or grab their prey. The Avocet, however, moves its sensitive bill from side-to-side through the water to find potential food. Look out for the amusing sight of waders using their feet to stir up the muddy bottom to disturb possible prey.

▲ **Hamerkop**
*Scopus umbretta* (56 cm) 81
These water birds, with their hammer-shaped heads, are usually found alone or in pairs. Their flattened beaks are well-adapted for catching frogs or carrying large sticks for building their huge nests.

◄ **Little Egret**
*Egretta garzetta* (64 cm) 67
These water birds have black legs with yellow feet and a plume on the back of their heads. They wade in shallow water where they hunt small animals such as tadpoles, fish and crabs.

**Grey Heron** ►
*Ardea cinerea*
(100 cm) 62
The large, long-legged Grey Herons have white heads and black eye-stripes which end in a wispy plume at the back of the head. They eat fish, frogs, crabs and insects.

◄ **Blacksmith Plover**
*Vanellus armatus*
Wader (30 cm) 258
Blacksmith Plovers are often seen in pairs or small groups. Their call sounds like a hammer on an anvil. They eat insects, worms and small molluscs. Their nests are lined, shallow depressions.

**▲ Three-banded Plover**
*Charadrius tricollaris*
Wader (18 cm) 249
This small bird is a
common resident with
double, black breast-
bands that make it
instantly identifiable. It
moves quickly along the
shores and shallows of
inland waters, on its own,
in pairs or small flocks.

**Ruff ▼**
*Philomachus pugnax*
(24 - 30 cm) (284)
The Ruff is a summer migrant found
around estuaries and
wetlands. It occurs
singly or in flocks,
and may be seen
wading about in shallow water
probing for invertebrates and
plant matter. The orange legs and
stout bill are diagnostic features
of the adults.

**◄ Wood Sandpiper**
*Tringa glareola*
(20 cm) 266
The Wood Sandpiper is recognised by
its conspicuous white eyebrow, white
speckles on its back, and green-tinged
legs. It is a common summer visitor, seen
foraging along estuaries and wetlands for
insects and other invertebrates.

**◄ Avocet**
*Recurvirostra
avosetta* Wader
(43 - 46 cm) 294
Avocets wade in
shallow water in small
flocks, sweeping their
beaks from side-to-side
over the surface to catch
aquatic animals. Their
nests are found on the
ground, near water.

**Whimbrel ►**
*Numenius phaeopus*
Wader (43 cm) 290
Whimbrels are shy birds,
usually seen alone or in
small groups. They mainly
eat crabs, prawns and shellfish.
They have down-curved bills and
two distinct stripes above each eye,
one pale and one dark.

**◄ Black-winged Stilt**
*Himantopus himantopus*
Wader (38 cm) 295
Occuring in small flocks, they feed early
or late in the day on insects and worms.
They nest in shallow hollows on
floating vegetation or small islands.

# FOREST

These birds use the canopies of the forest to feed and nest, and are therefore more difficult to see. When looking for forest birds, bear in mind that the greatest number are found around the edges or in clearings. This is because these places receive more light, and are where the birds can find warmth, visibility and a richer food source.

*Watch carefully and quietly for sudden movement, or flashes of colour which reveal the birds presence.*

**Red-billed Woodhoopoe ►**
*Phoeniculus purpureus*
(30 - 36 cm) 452
Red-billed Woodhoopoes are common, noisy birds, often found in groups. They can be seen examining the trunks and branches of trees looking for food such as nectar, insects, millipedes and lizards. They nest in holes in trees.

*(M)*

**◄ Paradise Flycatcher**
*Terpsiphone viridis*
(M 23 - 41 cm including tail;
F 16 - 18 cm) 710
In breeding season, the male has very long tail feathers. They call and flit about a lot, catching small insects on the wing. They usually nest in the fork of a tree.

**◄ Knysna Lourie**
*Tauraco corythaix*
(45 - 47 cm) 370
The red feathers on these birds' wings are more noticeable in flight. Their call is a trumpet-like *'woop, woop'*, followed by a growling *'korr, korr'*. They eat mainly fruit and build their nests from sticks.

**Sombre Bulbul ►**
*Andropadus importunus*
(19 - 23 cm) 572
The call of this bird is a distinctive *'weee-wee'* which ends in a drawn-out whistle. They mainly eat fruit and insects and their nests are built at the ends of branches.

**◄ Chorister Robin**
*Cossypha dichroa* (19 - 20 cm) 598
Keeping to the forest canopy, these robins are seldom seen. Their song is a melody of piping trills and whistles, often mimicking other birds. They eat mainly insects and nest in tree holes.

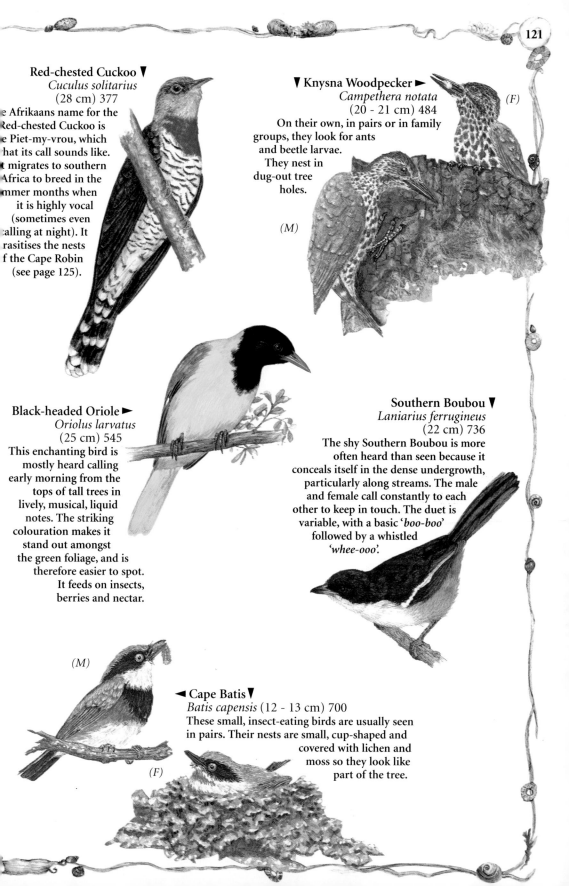

### Red-chested Cuckoo ▼
*Cuculus solitarius*
(28 cm) 377
e Afrikaans name for the
Red-chested Cuckoo is
e Piet-my-vrou, which
hat its call sounds like.
t migrates to southern
Africa to breed in the
mmer months when
it is highly vocal
(sometimes even
alling at night). It
rasitises the nests
f the Cape Robin
(see page 125).

### ▼ Knysna Woodpecker ►
*Campethera notata*
(20 - 21 cm) 484
(F)
On their own, in pairs or in family
groups, they look for ants
and beetle larvae.
They nest in
dug-out tree
holes.

(M)

### Black-headed Oriole ►
*Oriolus larvatus*
(25 cm) 545
This enchanting bird is
mostly heard calling
early morning from the
tops of tall trees in
lively, musical, liquid
notes. The striking
colouration makes it
stand out amongst
the green foliage, and is
therefore easier to spot.
It feeds on insects,
berries and nectar.

### Southern Boubou ▼
*Laniarius ferrugineus*
(22 cm) 736
The shy Southern Boubou is more
often heard than seen because it
conceals itself in the dense undergrowth,
particularly along streams. The male
and female call constantly to each
other to keep in touch. The duet is
variable, with a basic '*boo-boo*'
followed by a whistled
'*whee-ooo*'.

(M)

### ◄ Cape Batis ▼
*Batis capensis* (12 - 13 cm) 700
These small, insect-eating birds are usually seen
in pairs. Their nests are small, cup-shaped and
covered with lichen and
moss so they look like
part of the tree.

(F)

# FYNBOS

Fynbos provides a unique habitat for birds. It is not surprising therefore that several species occur nowhere else in the world, include the Cape Sugarbird, Orange-breasted Sunbird and Cape Francolin. Many fynbos plants are pollinated by birds such as the sunbirds and sugarbirds, which are attracted to the large amounts of sweet nectar produced by the flowers.

*When watching birds in fynbos, try to notice which bird pollinates which flower.*

◀ **Cape Sugarbird**
*Promerops cafer*
(M 37 - 44 cm; F 24 - 29 cm)
773
Sugarbirds are larger and less colourful than sunbirds. They mainly eat insects and nectar from Protea flowers. They breed during the winter and build cup-shaped nests in Proteas.

*(M)*

**Malachite Sunbird** ▶
*Nectarinia famosa*
(M 24 - 26 cm including tail; F 15 cm) 775
Often seen hovering above Aloe or Protea flowers, they eat insects, spiders and nectar. Their oval nests are built over water or in the bank of a dry ravine.

*(M)*

*(F)*

**Orange-breasted Sunbird** ▶
*Nectarinia violacea*
(M 17 cm; F 13 cm) 777
Usually occurring in pairs, they are active and noisy. They feed on nectar and insects caught on the wing. They nest in low bushes or in the tops of tall trees.

*(M)*

▲ **Lesser Double-collared Sunbird** ▶
*Nectarinia chalybea*
(11 - 13 cm) 783
These birds fly with rapid, swerving movements. They eat insects and nectar. The pear-shaped nest is suspended from the branch of a bush or small tree.

*(M)*

*(F)*

**Cape Canary** ▶
*Serinus canicollis*
(13 - 14 cm) 872
One of the best songsters in the fynbos is the Cape Canary. It is usually seen in flocks next to scrub areas where it forages on the ground or perches on the stems of seeding plants. The grey on the neck and shoulders is diagnostic.

**Grassbird ►**
*Sphenoeacus afer*
(19 - 23 cm) 661
When not hunting for
spiders and insects in the
dense vegetation, the
Grassbird is first seen
perching on top of a
grass stem or bush. It is
a fairly large, untidy
looking, streaky-
brown bird with
rufous crown
and a long
pointed tail.

**Spotted Prinia ►**
*Prinia maculosa*
(13 - 15 cm) 686
The Spotted Prinia forages
for insects low down in the
grass and bushes where it is
hard to see. If disturbed,
however, it perches on a
vantage point and flicks it
long tail up over its back
and calls *'kli-kli-kli-
krrrt-krrrt'*.

**Ground Woodpecker ▼**
*Geocolaptes olivaceus*
(25 - 30 cm) 480
Unlike other woodpeckers, they
forage on the ground, mainly
for ants. They have a
'guard' on duty to warn
them of danger. They
nest in holes dug in
river banks.

**◄ Cape Bulbul**
*Pyncnotus capensis*
(19 - 21 cm) 566
An endemic of the Cape
fynbos, the Cape Bulbul
is very vocal and
conspicuous, with
a diagnostic white
wattle around the
eye. It has a fast, bouncy flight, and is
often found in thickets. It feeds on
nectar and fruit.

**Victorin's Warbler ▼**
*Bradypterus victorini*
(15 - 17 cm) 641
An elusive bird, the Victorin's
Warbler is very difficult to spot.
It spends most its time
foraging between dense
vegetation in the
undergrowth or on the
ground. It is endemic
and confined to the
Cape fynbos.

**▼ Cape Francolin ►**
*Francolinus capensis*
(40 - 42 cm) 195
These birds are usually
found in thickets, in
pairs or in flocks. They
roost in trees and are very
noisy in the morning and
evening. They eat bulbs,
seeds, berries and insects.

*Sandbathing*

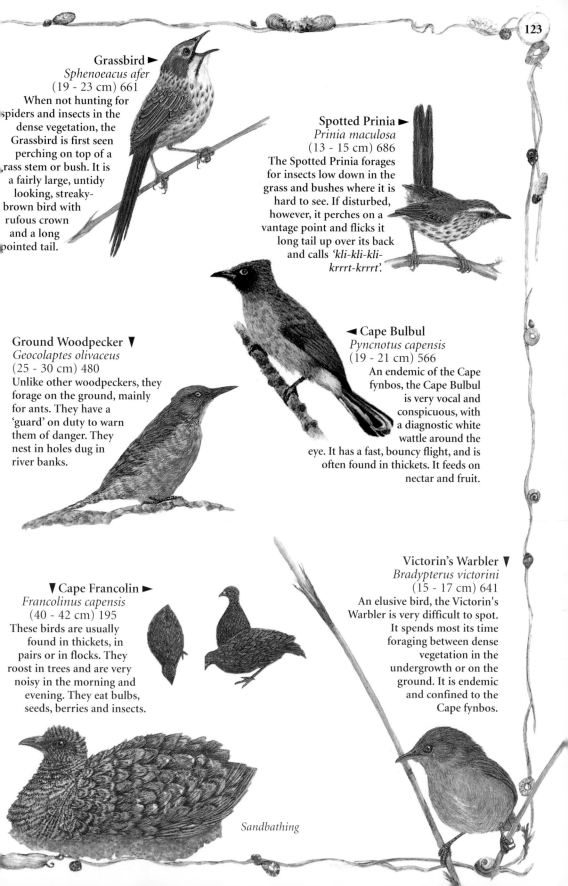

# OTHER COMMON BIRDS

These common birds occur in a wide variety of habitats, from forest to fynbos to coast, and some permanently live in our gardens at home. The Cape White-eye, Fiscal Shrike and Hadeda Ibis are well adapted to suburbia. The other birds require specific environmental conditions that urban areas cannot often provide, and they therefore do not occur there. The Forest Buzzard depends on forests for survival and will not occur in other habitats. Understanding the specific habitat requirements of any bird will assist with identification.

*Nest boxes and food trays will attract many garden birds. However planting trees that are indigenous to the area will establish long-term and healthier relationships with them.*

**Hadeda Ibis ▶**
*Bostrychia hagedash*
(76 cm) 94
Named after their unique call, Hadedas are found in groups, probing the ground for insects, spiders, snails and earthworms. Their nests look like platforms of sticks.

**◀ Helmeted Guineafowl**
*Numida meleagris*
(53 - 58 cm) 203
Usually in flocks, these birds wander a lot. They are good runners and scatter and fly up into trees when alarmed. They eat seeds, bulbs, insects and snails, and nest in hollows under bushes.

**Black-headed Heron ▶**
*Ardea melanocephala* (97 cm) 63
The elegant Black-headed Heron is a solitary feeder, eating frogs, rodents and small birds. The nests are large platforms of sticks.

**◀ Sacred Ibis**
*Threskiornis aethiopicus*
(89 cm) 91
They are usually seen in groups which fly in a 'V' formation. They walk with slow, careful steps as they feed, looking for insects, small mammals, frogs, young birds and birds' eggs.

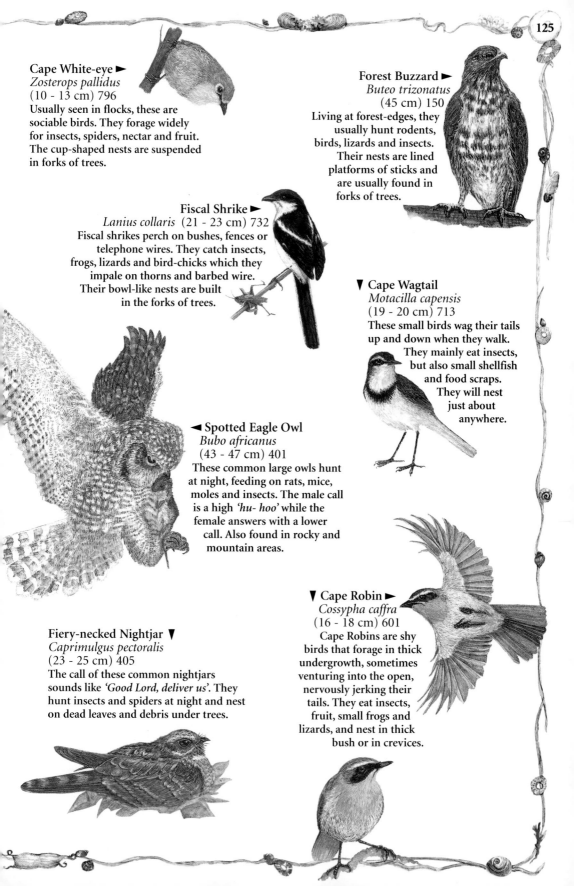

**Cape White-eye ►**
*Zosterops pallidus*
(10 - 13 cm) 796
Usually seen in flocks, these are
sociable birds. They forage widely
for insects, spiders, nectar and fruit.
The cup-shaped nests are suspended
in forks of trees.

**Forest Buzzard ►**
*Buteo trizonatus*
(45 cm) 150
Living at forest-edges, they
usually hunt rodents,
birds, lizards and insects.
Their nests are lined
platforms of sticks and
are usually found in
forks of trees.

**Fiscal Shrike ►**
*Lanius collaris* (21 - 23 cm) 732
Fiscal shrikes perch on bushes, fences or
telephone wires. They catch insects,
frogs, lizards and bird-chicks which they
impale on thorns and barbed wire.
Their bowl-like nests are built
in the forks of trees.

**▼ Cape Wagtail**
*Motacilla capensis*
(19 - 20 cm) 713
These small birds wag their tails
up and down when they walk.
They mainly eat insects,
but also small shellfish
and food scraps.
They will nest
just about
anywhere.

**◄ Spotted Eagle Owl**
*Bubo africanus*
(43 - 47 cm) 401
These common large owls hunt
at night, feeding on rats, mice,
moles and insects. The male call
is a high *'hu- hoo'* while the
female answers with a lower
call. Also found in rocky and
mountain areas.

**▼ Cape Robin ►**
*Cossypha caffra*
(16 - 18 cm) 601
Cape Robins are shy
birds that forage in thick
undergrowth, sometimes
venturing into the open,
nervously jerking their
tails. They eat insects,
fruit, small frogs and
lizards, and nest in thick
bush or in crevices.

**Fiery-necked Nightjar ▼**
*Caprimulgus pectoralis*
(23 - 25 cm) 405
The call of these common nightjars
sounds like *'Good Lord, deliver us'*. They
hunt insects and spiders at night and nest
on dead leaves and debris under trees.

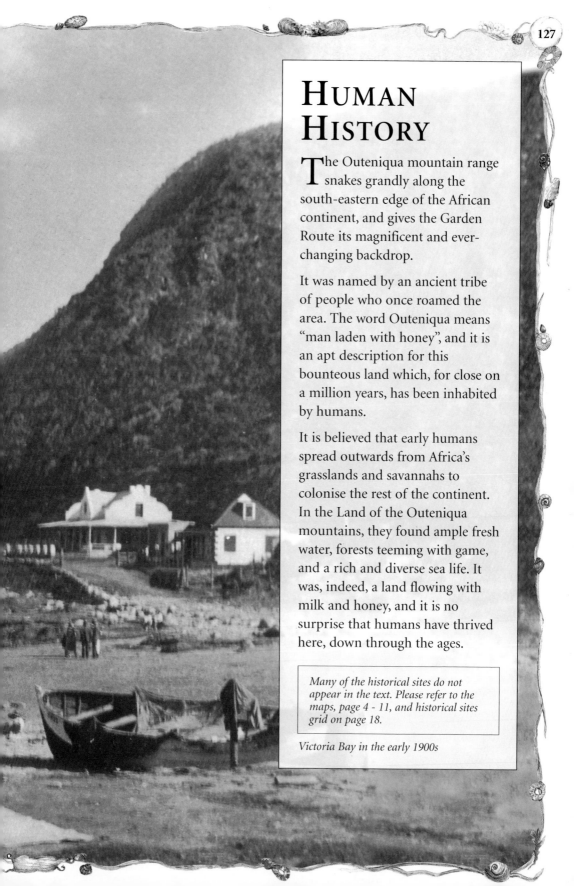

# HUMAN HISTORY

The Outeniqua mountain range snakes grandly along the south-eastern edge of the African continent, and gives the Garden Route its magnificent and ever-changing backdrop.

It was named by an ancient tribe of people who once roamed the area. The word Outeniqua means "man laden with honey", and it is an apt description for this bounteous land which, for close on a million years, has been inhabited by humans.

It is believed that early humans spread outwards from Africa's grasslands and savannahs to colonise the rest of the continent. In the Land of the Outeniqua mountains, they found ample fresh water, forests teeming with game, and a rich and diverse sea life. It was, indeed, a land flowing with milk and honey, and it is no surprise that humans have thrived here, down through the ages.

*Many of the historical sites do not appear in the text. Please refer to the maps, page 4 - 11, and historical sites grid on page 18.*

*Victoria Bay in the early 1900s*

# PEOPLE OF THE STONE AGE

Unlike modern settlers who, in just three short centuries, plundered much of what Jan van Riebeeck had described as 'the finest forests in the world', Stone Age people lived in harmony with their surroundings.

Able to gather firewood for fuel, hunt game in the forests, and harvest nuts, berries and roots, they also found many caves in the area which provided shelter and warmth. As archaeologists have proved, the next million years would see a slow development of more sophisticated ways of harvesting the bounty of nature.

*Stone tools*

### Earlier Stone A

The earliest evidence of people living in the southern Cape comes from stone implements of the Earlier Stone Age that date back to about one million years ago. We cannot be more precise because not much remains after such a long time. Usually it is only the stone tools that survive to show that people lived along the coast. There is no evidence that they ate fish and shellfish, although they certainly hunted game and ate wild plants.

*Early Stone Age m*

*Collecting berries from the early forests*

*Early Stone Age people w have utilised forests like t for collecting f*

*Nelson Bay Cave, rich with revealing middens*

## Middle Stone Age

The history of people in the southern Cape is closely linked to global changes in sea level. This level rose and fell with melting and freezing of polar ice caps, in cycles that lasted about 100 000 years. About 125 000 years ago, when the climate was a little warmer and the sea level was higher than it is at present, Middle Stone Age people began enjoying shellfish as part of their diet. Piles of shells that were thrown away after the shellfish were eaten (shell middens) have been preserved in caves on the coast.

*A great number of different shells have been found in middens all over this area.*

Shell middens that date from about 40 000 to 30 000 years ago, are now beneath the sea. This is because the sea level was lower then, and the coastline was as much as 100 km south of its present position. The colder climate at that time also led to some mammals having a larger body size. The bones of animals hunted by the people living inland show evidence of some 'giant' forms. For example, there were giant Cape horse / zebra and giant buffalo that were at least fifty percent larger than the similar modern species.

*Fish gorges (hooks)*

## Later Stone Age

12 000 years ago, the sea level rose close to its present position. Again there is plenty of evidence in the area of the activities of Later Stone Age people. Fishing and shellfish collecting, as well as hunting of small antelope, and collecting of ground game like tortoise and hare, were common. Later Stone Age people were the ancestors of the Khoesan and were technologically more advanced than the people of the Middle Stone Age. They made stone sinkers and bone points (or gorges) for fishing, and bows and arrows for hunting. They also made stone weights for sticks to help the women dig up roots, bulbs and corms.

*Later Stone Age people were ancestors of the Khoesan.*

*Sinkers found at Nelson Bay Cave*

# HUNTER-GATHERERS AND HERDERS

The sea has been the centre of life in this area from the earliest times. The archaeological record shows that hunter-gatherers, living on the Southern Cape coast, used the sea as their main food source. The story of human settlement on this coast goes back at least 100 000 years. More recently, in the last 10 000 years, hunter-gatherers probably moved to the coast for the mild winter after spending the summer inland.

It was not until 2 000 years ago that people, who lived a different way of life from the hunter-gatherers, entered this area. Archaeologists have found evidence that, from that time, herding people used the southern Cape coast seasonally.

*Watsonia corms, page 93, an important food source.*

*Bored stone used as a weight when digging*

*Gatherer women collecting seeds and corms.*

### Hunter-gatherers

These people lived by hunting small mammals, and by fishing and gathering roots, bulbs and seeds. Archaeologists have found many artifacts that help us to understand how hunter-gatherers lived in this coastal area. There are a number of archaeological sites on the Garden Route that are easy to visit: Cape St. Blaize Cave at Mossel Bay which used to have a shell midden but has been largely destroyed (see site 7 on page 5); Nelson Bay Cave on the Robberg Peninsula (see site 31 on pages 9 and 10); and Matjes River Rock Shelter near Keurboomstrand (see site 39 on page 10). The fish traps at Still Bay and Rein's Coastal Nature Reserve (see sites 1 and 4 on page 4) are fascinating at low spring tide.

*Shell pend⋯ foun⋯ Nelson⋯ Cave. Sim⋯ pendants h⋯ been foun⋯ the inland sit⋯ Melkhoutbo⋯ north of⋯ Elizab⋯*

*Rock painting found in the area*

*Thou, O Tsui-G⋯*
*Thou father of the fathe⋯*
*Thou our fath⋯*
*Let the thunder cloud strea⋯*
*Please let our flocks li⋯*
*Please let us also li⋯*
*I am so very weak inde⋯*
*From thi⋯*
*From hung⋯*
*That I may eat field fru⋯*
*Art thou not then our fath⋯*
*The father of the fathe⋯*
*Thou Tsui G⋯*
*That we may praise th⋯*
*That we may give thee⋯*
*retu⋯*
*Thou father of the fathe⋯*
*Thou our Lo⋯*
*Thou, O Tsui-G⋯*

*This is a hymn of praise to⋯ Khoekhoe God Tsui-Goa!⋯ hymn was first translated⋯ recorded in the 1700s by Geo⋯ Schmidt, a missionary who c⋯ to work among the Khoekh⋯ One of the field fruits mentio⋯ in the hymn would have b⋯ Indian Grass. The bulb⋯ collected by hunter-gathere⋯ and herders and later by⋯ Dutch settlers who called⋯ them 'uintjies'.*

*Painting tool*

*Fish traps (Still Bay), see sites 1 and 4 on page 2.*

## Religion and Art

*Artist's rendition of a rock painting*

The area is rich in hunter-gatherer rock paintings. Most of these are in museums or on private land and are not accessible. The paintings of hunter-gatherers have a deep religious significance. They record their experiences of trances, which were important religious events. Like hunter-gatherers everywhere, those living along the southern Cape coast depicted animals in their trance paintings that were significant to their survival in that area. Certain animals, particularly the eland, were thought to be more powerful than others. The whale painting shown here is from a stone found near Storms River Mouth. The person 'swimming' with dolphins comes from a stone found at Klasies River Cave. Evidence of shellfish, fish caught with hooks and nets, seal bones and whale bones (probably from beached whales) show how much these people took advantage of the resources of the sea.

## Herders

Hunter-gatherers kept sheep and cattle and moved to this coast from inland for the winter months. These people called themselves Khoekhoe (pronounced koi-koi) which means 'men of men'. There is evidence of interaction between herder and hunter-gatherer societies. Herders sometimes relied on hunting, fishing and gathering to supplement their diet. Hunter-gatherers often worked as servants for the herders. Both groups also had contact with Xhosa Iron Age farmers who lived to the east, within the summer rainfall area, where their crops of sorghum and millet grew well.

*Pottery shards*

*The Khoekhoe made pots like these for storing milk. Pieces of the pots can still be found in the area.*

One of the sources of evidence we have about these herding people are accounts and drawings made by travellers from Europe in the seventeenth and eighteenth centuries. Although these are not always accurate, because of the travellers' ignorance and prejudice, they do provide us with a rich source of evidence about the herders' way of life ... *"Their riches consist of cattle, such as oxen and sheep ... If they will slaughter a beast they choose always the worst and thinnest, saying that it would be a pity to kill a fat animal".* Vermeulen, 1668, quoted in Raven-Hart, Major, R, Cape of Good Hope 1652-1702, the First Fifty years, 2 vols, Balkema, Cape Town, 1970.

*Distribution of herders in the seventeenth and eighteenth centuries*

*Koekhoe huts*

*"They have no houses but live in little huts which they make from bent sticks or hoops. They hang reed mats on the sticks. These huts are usually set ten or twelve together in a circle, within which their cattle stand by night, and by day roam widely round to graze. As soon as they see that their cattle have no more pasture, they take down their huts, lay the hoops on their pack oxen, and set them up elsewhere, wherever they find good grass."* Hoffmann, 1672, quoted in Raven-Hart, Major, R, Cape of Good Hope 1652-1702, the First Fifty years, 2 vols, Balkema, Cape Town, 1970.

# TRAVELLERS AND SHIPWRECKS

The natural advantages of the coastal area included wide half-heart bays that made ideal harbours for passing ships. The fresh water and trade for meat with the Khoekhoe first brought the sea-faring European explorers on land. When the Dutch East India Company took over control of the trade route to the East, it set up a refreshment station at Cape Town in the seventeenth century. It was not long before travellers from the new settlement became aware of the riches of the southern Cape coast – today's Garden Route.

### Portuguese travellers

The search for a sea passage from Europe to the East was the reason why Portuguese sailors passed this coast. In 1488 Bartolomeu Dias stopped to get fresh water at the place we call Mossel Bay today. A replica of his ship can be seen here in the Maritime Museum in the Bartolomeu Dias centre (see site 8 on page 5). Dias left the following account of his journey and of his meetings with the Khoekhoe herders ...

*Dutch East Ind
Company se*

*"We sighted land in a bay which we called the Bahia dos Vaqueiros, because of the many cows seen there, watched by their herdsmen. And since they had no language which could b understood, we could have no speech with them; but rath they drove off their cattle inland, as if terrified of such a new matter, so that we could learn no more of them."*
Bartolomeu Dias, 1488, quoted in Raven-Hart, Major, R, Cape of Good Hope 1652-1702, the First Fifty years, 2 vols, Balkema, Cape Town, 1970.

*17th century navigational instrument*

*Replica of Bartholomeu Dias' sh*

From this time onward many Portuguese ships stopped on their way to the East to collect water from the Hartenbos River that runs into Mossel Bay. They often traded beads and buttons for cattle and sheep with Khoekhoe herders.

*Early sailors battling high seas*

*Beads us
for tradi*

**Shipwreck**

The east coast of southern Africa was not safe for sailing ships and several Portuguese vessels sunk there in the fifteenth and sixteenth centuries. In 1630 the San Gonzales was on her way back to Portugal from India, when her captain stopped in the bay, called Plettenberg Bay today, to repair some leaks. Before the repairs could be done, the ship

*White Milkwood (page 96)*

*This White Milkwood was probably the first 'post office' on the southern Cape coast (see site 9 on page 5). In 1501 a Portuguese sailor João da Nova, found a letter left by another sailor in a boot hanging from this tree. The tree became known as the Post Office Tree. You can still see one of these trees in the same spot at Mossel Bay today.*

sank. 150 sailors drowned, but 100 swam to shore and lived in the Piesang Valley for eight months. While there, they built two boats with the remains of the San Gonzales and timber from the forest trees. One of the sailors left an account of their time on this coast ...

*"We built habitations of wood ... and sowed various seeds to enjoy the fruit thereof, such as pumpkins, melons, onions and coriander ... the soil is excellent, and free from stones, though there are various hills. These, as also the valleys, abound with verdure and plants with sweet smelling flowers. The trees are numerous and large. In all parts it is watered by voluminous rivers and abundant and fine springs ... There is an infinite number of wild animals of extraordinary size, such as deer, wolves, seals, buffaloes, wild boars, monkeys and also tigers and elephants."* Theal G M, Records of Southern Eastern Africa, 8 vols, Struik reprint, Cape Town, 1964

*Quill pen*

The sailors eventually set out in the boats they had built, leaving behind a stone as a reminder of the original shipwreck. Known as the Van Plettenberg stone, it is housed in the Cape Town Museum, with a replica at Beacon Island, Plettenberg Bay (see site 36 on page 10). They were eventually picked up by other Portuguese vessels. Tragically, one of these ships sank with the shipwrecked sailors aboard, just as the ship entered the harbour at Lisbon.

**Travellers from Cape Town**

Many travellers wrote accounts of their journey through this area. The most colourful account is perhaps that written by the Frenchman Le Vaillant. One of the stories he tells is of his narrow

*Le Vaillant's book*

escape with an elephant in the Knysna Forest. The wounded elephant charged him, and he escaped only by lying low on the ground. He and some Khoekhoe men then killed the elephant and, as this diary entry shows, made good use of the animal. This aimless hunting of the elephant continued well into the nineteenth century and eventually led to the animals' virtual extinction in the forest.

*"We took such parts of the elephant as we wanted, particularly the fat, for greasing our wheels and traces and for burning. I had no cotton, and was obliged to make use of my cravats."* Le Vaillant

*Knysna Elephant, Loxodonta africana. Although elephants do not normally live in forests, hunting activities of the past forced those that remained into the Knysna Forest.*

# NINETEENTH CENTURY

Throughout the nineteenth century, people armed with the tools of the Industrial Revolution left Europe to find their fortunes on new continents. The natural advantages and resources of the Garden Route made it prime land for settlement and exploitation.

However, despite brief attempts at timber, gold and whaling, it never developed as a major urban or industrial area. This was because of the severe restrictions to travel presented by the deep gorges along the rivers, and the high ranges of the mountains running parallel to the coast.

## Woodcutters in the Forest

In an age before oil wells and coal mines, timber was practically the only source of fuel available, so it was inevitable that the mighty forests lining the Garden Route were hungrily eyed by early settlers. Many hoped there would be easy money to be made in feeding this insatiable hunger for wood, and the first woodcutters were recorded at work in the forests in 1711. During the next two centuries, their numbers grew rapidly, even though most of them actually lived a poor and miserable existence, cut off from all civilisation. In spite of this, the woodcutters developed a strong cultural identity, and added a unique and distinctive flavour to the area. Indeed, it was not until 1939 that private woodcutting was finally banned altogether in the Outeniqua forests.

*"The great bundles of logs were fastened together with chains, and attached to oxen. In front into the sea swam the touleier - a strong-swimming ox - while from behind other men drove the rest of the oxen … until they were alongside the boats and the logs loaded."*
*"Plettenberg Bay to Knysna – a trip through history," in Kelley-Paterson, E., Looking Back, June 1971.*

*Black Stinkwood, (page 85)*

*Branches shown here are some of the tree species utilised by the woodcutters.*

*Percheron horses also dragged logs from the forest.*

*A woodcutters saw used in this period*

Small Ironwood (page 85)

"Plettenberg Bay to Knysna – a trip
through history", in Kelley-Patterson, E.,
Looking Back, June 1971 "The woods
are very thick and produce some of
the tallest trees I ever beheld … The
mountains are extremely steep and
many of the most stately trees grow
out of the naked strata of the rocks …
These woods have their beginning to
the north of Mossel Bay and extend
st 120 miles to the east ending at a place
l Zitsicamma. Between the woods and the
n Ocean lies an extensive plain inhabited by
peans who traffic mostly in wood which they
in planks to the Cape."
enant William Paterson, 1777, in Paterson,
W. Paterson's Cape Travels
1777-1779, ed. Forbes V.S.
and Rourke J, Brenthurst,
Johannesburg, 1980.

*Belvidere Church*

### Settlers

Off the main Knysna road (see
site 26 on page 8) you will find a
lone tombstone that holds this
inscription …"In memory of
George Rex, proprietor and
founder of Knysna." Rex is probably one of the most famous
of the settlers who came to this area in the nineteenth
century. Legend claims that he was the son of George III
of England and a Quaker woman. Whether this is
true or not, we know he arrived in Knysna to
settle on the farm Melkhoutkraal in 1804. He
brought with him his family, masons, carpenters,
bricklayers, a blacksmith, 100 slaves and a
plumber, all in 166 wagons.

One of the best known landmarks left by Rex's
family, is the beautiful Belvidere Church
consecrated in 1855 (see site 19 on page 8). The
church was built by Rex's son-in-law, Thomas Henry Duthie.
Duthie fell in love with Caroline Rex while on a hunting
expedition in the forest. Duthie returned to settle at Belvidere
where he built the church and also the very beautiful village
of Knysna.

nents from Thesen's
any, from the early 1900s

*George Rex's
gravestone*

IN MEMORY OF GEORGE REX ESQUIRE PROPRIETOR AND FOUNDER OF KNYSNA, DIED 3RD APRIL 1839

*Small-leaved
Yellowwood
(page 85)*

In 1869 another family, who had an important impact on
the area, arrived in Knysna. The Thesen family left Norway
in their ship the Albatross, on their way to settle in New Zealand.
They stopped in Knysna to deliver cargo and decided to stay.
hesens became involved in a number of business activities, including shipping, commerce
mber. To this day the name Thesen is associated with timber in the Knysna area.

# NINETEENTH CENTURY

As the nineteenth century progressed, settlers continued to be drawn by the promise of a better life in the furthest reaches of the African continent. Towns like Plettenburg Bay and Knysna were established, and while they would never play a major role in South Africa's economic development, the prosperity of the area was assured.

### The Forests

The increasing demand for timber began to threaten the forests, and as early as 1803, the traveller Lichtenstein warned of the serious depletion of the indigenous trees ...

*"Even here, the timber begins so far to fail that whereas formerly they did not cut any for beams less than 30 fe high, none are now found except in the deep kloof."*
Lichtenstein, 1803, in Lichtenstein, H, Travels in Southe
Africa, 1803, 1804, 1805, 2 vols, Van Riebeeck Society,
Cape Town, VRC 10/11, 1928, 1930

*Gold nuggets*

*Sifting pan used by the diggers*

*Felled alien trees*

### The Great Fire

Disaster struck the forest in 1869 when a great fire raged for weeks from Mossel Bay to Humansdorp. After the fire, the only trees that remained were those growing in the deep kloofs. It was only now that the authorities began to consider the conservation of the forests. The first conservator was appointed in 1874, and in 1880, a French forestry expert made a misguided attempt to conserve the forest. Although stopped the felling of trees in some ar he also planted many exotic species including pines a gums. These alien tre overran the indigeno vegetation and, today over a century later, efforts to clear these aliens are still ongoing in m areas.

*Cluster
(page*

*Gold diggers camp in the 19th Centuary*

*Gold nuggets*

*Millwood Museum*

## ...ggers, Whalers ...d the Railway

...was not only timber
...t drew people to the
...thern Cape Coast.
...ere was gold too! In
...6, a gold nugget was
...nd at Millwood in the
...ysna forest. Diggers
...m all over the world
...ived to find their
...tunes in the forests.
...1888, a small town had
...wn at Millwood, but
...great goldfields were
...nd. When news of the
...d-finds on the Reef
...ne to this area, most of the diggers left, and Millwood became a ghost town. Visit the site
...he town today and you will find an old building, Monks' Store, and signs to indicate where the
...ets once were. Close to the town in the forest are old mine shafts and machinery hidden now
in the dense undergrowth.

*...ly whaling off the Cape coast*

Apart from wood and gold from the forests, modern settlers also tried to take advantage of other riches of the area. In 1912, a Norwegian whaling company set up a whaling station at Beacon Island (see site 32 on page 10). From here the boats set out into the Indian Ocean in search of the Southern Right Whale that frequents these waters. Whaling operations stopped in 1916. Since the moratorium on whaling was instituted in 1983, the whale population has increased world-wide by about 7% each year.

*Metal plate of the Outeniqua steam train*

...e inaccessibility of the area continued to prevent many people from exploring
...coast and forests. It was only when the railway line was built, that more visitors
...quented the southern Cape. In 1928, a railway line from George to Knysna was
...npleted. You can relive the excitement of this moment by travelling the same
...e on the steam train, the Outeniqua Choo-tjoe (see site 22 on page 8).

*Outeniqua Choo-tjoe*

# HUMAN IMPACT

Humans are as much a part of the environment as any other living organism. However, we are the most destructive. Many natural areas of South Africa are under threat from the increase in human activities – from recreational to commercial – and the Garden Route is no exception. The following information will help you to preserve this spectacular part of the country, and to minimize your impact on the area.

### Fires

Natural fires, such as those caused by lightning, play a role in shaping the landscape. Unnatural, runaw̶ fires during the hot, dry summers can devastate the environment. If you wish to light fires for picnicking purposes, do so only in designated places, and be su̶ to extinguish them when you leav̶

*Many fynbos plants, like the King Protea (page 91) need natural fires, in the correct season to enable regeneration.*

*Fires are a natural occurence, unless started by hum̶*

Buy your own wood for making fires. Collecting of firewood in natural areas, including forests and dunes, is prohibited. Dead wood forms an important part of the food-web and is home to many small creatures.

*Rhinoceros Beetles (p̶ 103) use decomposin̶ vegetation as breedin̶ sites, and are import̶ in the natural cycle.*

*Excessive use of recreational areas can have a detrimental effect on the environment, for example overfishing. Please clean up after visiting, so that you don't harm the wildlife, and so that others may enjoy the Garden Route after you.*

## ...ter

...man activity generates
...enormous amount of
...r that is not only
...entially hazardous to
...dlife and people, but also
...ils the natural beauty of
... environment. Before
... throw your litter on the
...und, consider that it
...es 100 to 400 years for
...s to disintegrate, and
...to 30 years for plastic
...decompose! If there are
...bins provided in the
..., please take your litter
...h you and consider
...ycling it.

*This unique beauty is worthy of our care*

## ...ound disturbance

...cially constructed paths and roadways have been created in many
...s to protect the natural vegetation and wildlife from destruction, and
...ecrease soil erosion. When walking, hiking or driving, please stick to
...marcated areas to avoid destroying sensitive plants, animals and soil.
...king of plants along public roads and in nature reserves is prohibited.
...wers are the sex organs of plants that create the next generation. So
admire them, but don't pick them.

*Picking flowers, like the Arum Lily (page 89), spoils the natural beauty and destroys the habitats of other living creatures, like the Arum Lily Frog (page 109).*

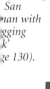

### Ancient History

If you are visiting areas with rock paintings,
archaeological sites or other historical monuments, please consider them
part of your natural heritage. To deface or remove any part of these ancient
implements is a crime and spoils them for future generations.

### Offroad Vehicles and Power Boats

These forms of recreation are very popular in South Africa. However, their
impact on the environment can be devastating. Water pollution, noise
pollution and the destruction of natural terrain can permanently damage
plant and animal life. Please be sure to familiarise yourself with the
guidelines and regulations before entering natural areas.
Enjoy, but don't destroy our Garden Route!

*...k painting ...San ...nan with ...gging ...k' ...ge 130).*

*Natural foodchains are dependant on a healthy, pollution-free environment, for example the White Steenbras (page 73) that feeds on prawns in estuaries.*

*Boating and ...yfishing ...Knysna Lagoon*

*...d ...wn ...ge 77)*

# HUMAN IMPACT

## ALIEN ANIMALS AND PLANTS

An alien species is a plant or animal which does not naturally occur in a defined area but which has been introduced from elsewhere by humans. An invasive (invader) species is usually an alien plant or animal which is capable of displacing indigenous species and causing irreversible changes. This is because there are no natural predators or control measures so it can reproduce and spread more rapidly.

In many areas, invasive alien plants such as pines, Hakeas and Acacias, dominate the natural fynbos vegetation in the southern Cape.

Fynbos is the most water-efficient vegetation type, and therefore allows maximum water to run-off into dams and rivers. Most aliens use enormous amounts of water and therefore limit species diversity and reduce the amount of water run-off considerably. Because of the aliens and the growing human population, a serious shortage of water is predicted for the future in this area.

◄ **Argentine Ant**
Linepithema humile Insect (3 m
The Argentine Ant invades areas of
fynbos. Unlike indigenous ants, they eat oily pa
of the seeds on the soil-surface, leaving the seeds expo:
and vulnerable. Re-generation of those plants that dep
on ants becomes much less successful. It may even res
in certain species being threatened with extinction.

◄ **European Starling**
*Stunus vulgaris*
Bird (20 - 22 cm) 757
A cocky, quarrelsome bird that was
introduced to Cape Town by Cecil John
Rhodes in 1899, and is now well established
the southern Cape. It inhabits urban areas a
farmyards where it often occurs in flocks of
hundreds. It is generally disliked because it
tends to displace other birds from town garde
and carries lice and mites. The European
Starling feeds on fruit,
seeds, insects and food-scraps
discarded by humans.

**Mosquito Fish** ►
*Gambusia affinis*
Fish (6 cm)
Originally from North
America, these fish were
introduced for mosquito control and as
food for bass. As they feed on larvae of
other fish, they are threatening
indigenous fish populations.

◄ **Largemouth Bass**
*Micropterus salmoides*
Fish (60 cm)
Originally from North
America, these fish were introduced
as popular freshwater gamefish.
They have caused lots of damage to
indigenous fish populations.

▼ **Mozambique Tilapia**
*Oreochromis mossambicus*
Fish (40 cm)
Introduced to the
southern Cape from
south-east Africa, these
fish live in rivers, lakes,
lagoons and estuaries. They
feed mainly on algae, and dead
plant material.

**Bluegill Sunfish** ►
*Lepomis macrochirus*
Fish (20 cm)
Originally from North
America, these fish were
introduced as fodder fish
for bass. They are now a
serious pest as they compete
with indigenous fish.

◄ **Port Jackson** ▲
*Acacia saligna* Tree (9 m)
This invader was brought in from Australia. It now occurs commonly in very dense thickets, especially along river-valleys at the expense of our indigenous vegetation.

**Rooikrans** ►
*Acacia cyclops*
Tree (3 - 5 m)
An unwelcome bushy tree that has narrow leaves and small, yellow flowers. Its seed-pods are coiled and the seeds, red with black centres, look like 'red eyes'. It was introduced from Australia, and grows in dense thickets which invade the indigenous vegetation.

▼ **Black Wattle** ►
*Acacia mearnsii* Tree (10 m)
The unwelcome Black Wattle has black, stringy bark, dark-green, feathery leaves and small, yellow flowers. It was introduced from Australia for the commercial use of its bark in the tanning industry. It now forms dense stands along river valleys throughout the southern Cape. This makes it difficult for indigenous plants to grow.

**Blue Gum** ▼
*Eucalyptus globulus*
Tree (70 m)
The Blue Gum was introduced to South Africa in 1828. The bark was traditionally used for timber, fuel, windbreaks, shade and ornaments. It was once planted extensively, but has however been superseded by species which are faster-growing and more resistant to fungus and insect attack. Noble, giant specimens still remain throughout the country as landmarks of early settlers.

◄ **Silky Hakea**
*Hakea sericea*
Tree (2,5 m)
This invader is an erect, single-stemmed shrub. Brought in from Australia, infestations now occur on all the major coastal ranges in the southern Cape. It poses a threat to the unique mountain fynbos which it smothers entirely. Conservation organisations spend millions of rands annually in an attempt to bring this plant under control.

◄ **Cluster Pine** ▼
*Pinus pinaster* Tree (30 m)
Pine trees were introduced to South Africa for their valuable soft wood. The Cluster Pine, introduced from the Mediterranean countries, has 'escaped' from plantations and is now threatening the natural plants growing in the southern Cape.

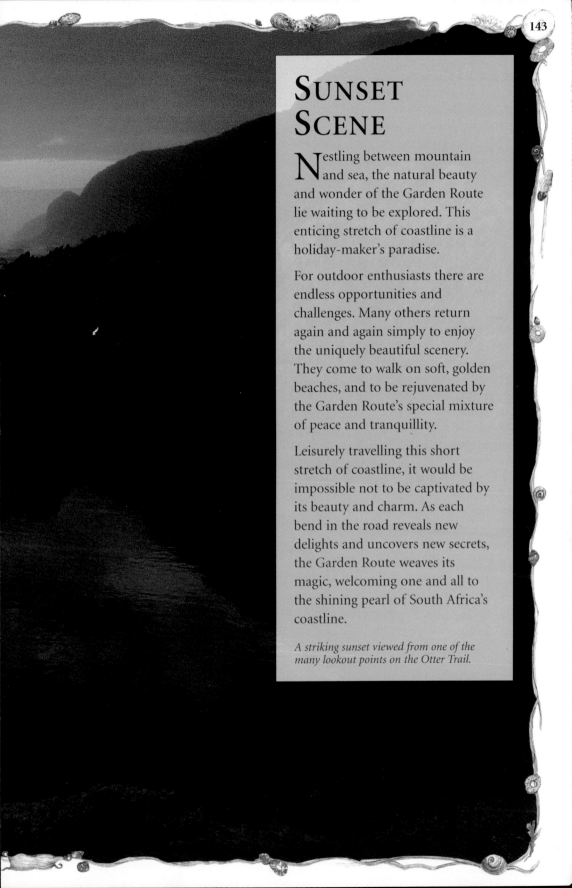

# SUNSET SCENE

Nestling between mountain and sea, the natural beauty and wonder of the Garden Route lie waiting to be explored. This enticing stretch of coastline is a holiday-maker's paradise.

For outdoor enthusiasts there are endless opportunities and challenges. Many others return again and again simply to enjoy the uniquely beautiful scenery. They come to walk on soft, golden beaches, and to be rejuvenated by the Garden Route's special mixture of peace and tranquillity.

Leisurely travelling this short stretch of coastline, it would be impossible not to be captivated by its beauty and charm. As each bend in the road reveals new delights and uncovers new secrets, the Garden Route weaves its magic, welcoming one and all to the shining pearl of South Africa's coastline.

*A striking sunset viewed from one of the many lookout points on the Otter Trail.*

# INDEX

*Striped Mouse,*
*page 104*

*Erica versicolor, page 90*

*Fiery-necked Nightjar, page 125*

# NOTES